Global Adventures in Style

Paraíso de la Bonita.

Global Adventures in Style

Dr. Jill Nash and Carlo Nash

Jetty at Ambergris Caye

Introduction

Travelling for us is about adventures. Whether sight-seeing in Beijing, wine-tasting in New Zealand or simply relaxing outside a café in Rome, experiencing a travel adventure shouldn't mean that you have to compromise on style or comfort. There are comfortable ways to get to your destination, stylish places to stay and delectable places to eat.

During our travel adventures, we became dissatisfied by the lack of information on luxurious and stylish places to stay that also suited a 'backpack' type adventure traveller. We found such hotels were usually overlooked by guidebooks; which left us to research for ourselves the best places to stay in each country, whilst still enjoying us the freedom to explore like a backpacker.

Following our first trip, the two conflicting themes became apparent, explore like a backpacker but travel in style. The best of both worlds. Luxury Backpackers is not just about travelling, and it is not just about 'nice' places to stay either. It is about seeking adventures and travel experiences in style and searching for the best that each country has to offer. I guess you could call us 'grown-up backpackers'.

Luxury Backpackers is for any type of luxury explorer, whether you are travelling for three weeks or three years or whether you are 25 or 65. We hope you enjoy our first book, 'Global adventures in Style' which covers an inspiring variety of countries. Look out for other books in this series of adventures in style.

Jill & Carlo

P.S Look for our personal star picks - these are places we have each had incredible experiences and would return to again and again.

Before you start...
what kind of Luxury
Backpacker are you?

Action Hero

Nature Lover

Culture Vulture

Beach Bum

Rest + Relaxation

City Slicker

Preface

It was one of those Road to Damascus moments. There I was lying in some flea-infested pit of a hotel room when I was struck by a blinding flash of inspiration. The room was an archetypal backpacker's hell-hole. It was damp and dirty. The mosquito net was full of holes, the fan didn't work and there was no window. And there was no running water. Then I went down with food poisoning. Why was I staying in this dump?

Such incidences are supposed to be all part of backpacking and the curious ethos that unless you're staying in some horrible hotel, it's somehow not an authentic experience. As I lay there, writhing in discomfort, I began to wonder, since when did backpacking become synonymous with having a bad time?

I love the spontaneity of travelling, the freedom of going where you want to go, the chance to act on a whim. The best knowledge is always gained locally and there is always an abundance of it. But if you're on a fixed schedule with confirmed bookings, you can't go off and stay in that lodge by the waterfall you just heard about, or visit that street festival in a nearby town. Having to turn down opportunities like this is intensely frustrating. "Next time," we kid ourselves.

But how do you get the balance right between spontaneity and avoiding the kind of hotels where room service is the person who kills the cockroaches?

Fortunately as Jill and Carlo Nash show in this wonderfully inspiring book, you don't have to sacrifice comfort and style when you go travelling. From the beaches of Belize to the bars of Beijing they have scoured the world and selected some of the world's great destinations to visit, whether you're looking for a rainforest adventure or a chilled time tasting wine.

I learnt to surf in Costa Rica and stayed in a hotel just by the beach which I'd heard about from another traveller. In New Zealand I found one of the most inspiring landscapes I've ever come across and didn't need to book anywhere in advance. (It was in winter though, an amazing time to visit - the whole country was blanketed in snow.) There are some ground rules - like booking your first week in advance - but leave it open beyond that and you will never look back. Be prepared however. You can't avoid some uncomfortable experiences. The last time I was in China, I was served chilli stir fry for breakfast.

Tarquin Cooper
Adventure Travel Writer

Top. South Island scenery.
Bottom. Surfing in Costa Rica.

🗒 Top 3 adventures

1. Adventure sports in New Zealand.
Take your pick of adventure sports from the country that gave birth to bungee jumping and the extreme sport revolution. For a real flavour of the country's awe-inspiring landscape, go hiking in South Island.

Top tip: Avoid the bustling town of Queenstown and stay in Wanaka.

2. Learning to surf on Costa Rica's Pacific coast. Wake up to the best coffee in the world and enjoy beautiful sunshine, great beaches and perfect rollers off the ocean. All this is found in a Central American country that's an oasis of peace and civilisation.

Top tip: Fly to the west coast in a small aircraft from San José.

3. Driving the Friendship Highway. Tibet Roads don't get much more spectacular than this. The Friendship Highway crosses the Himalayas from Lhasa to Nepal, and passes scenery that will take your breath away – if the thin air at this altitude hasn't already.

Top tip: Start your journey in Beijing on the new express train.

Costa Rican Jungle, Courtesy of Getty Images

COSTA RICA

San José | Nicoya Peninsula | Arenal | Tortuguero

COSTA RICA ● ● ●

Lago de Nicaragua

Caribbean Sea

The Northern Zone

Guanacaste & the Northwest — Arenal ● — La Fortuna

Tortuguero ●

The Caribbean Coast

Nicoya Peninsula

Nicoya ●

San José ●

Central Highlands

Central Pacific

South Central Costa Rica

Golfo Dulce & Peninsula de Osa

Pacific Ocean

🏆 Why is this place so special?

Costa Rica is truly an incredible and inspiring place to visit. It has wondrous wildlife, amazing beaches and some active volcanoes. Don't just take our word for it - as many as 1.5 million tourists visit the country every year.

Many travellers come to Costa Rica to experience its wildlife. The country covers just 0.1% of the planet's landmass, yet it is home to around 5% of the world's species of animals. Its coastlines with the Caribbean Sea and the Pacific Ocean offer a splendid mix of exotic animals, coral reefs and marine life - including rare species of dolphins and Manatees.

Culturally, there are some fascinating museums - which feature pre-Columbian artefacts - and interesting markets that sell unusual herbal remedies. You can also take a tour which explores Costa Rica's coffee industry - a vital contributor to the country's economy.

There is a lot to do for those who love outdoor adventure. Costa Rica's 26 national parks provide an excellent opportunity for rambling, its rivers offer exhilarating white water rafting, while its waterfalls yield superb abseiling and swimming. Also, the coasts boast some world-class surfing spots.

Costa Rica has developed into a tourist friendly hotspot in recent years. It is a relatively safe and easy place to explore and is suitable for independent travellers as well as for groups. The country is ideally situated to allow you to explore its neighbouring countries, such as Panama, Belize and Guatemala, and flights to these destinations are quick and inexpensive. A week or ten days should be long enough time to explore the wildlife and still have time to relax on a beach.

From top to bottom. Rapelling down the waterfalls in Arenal, Catching the most poisonous snake in Central America the Fer-de-lance, Watching the active volcano from a bathtub in Arenal.

Interestingly, Costa Rica has a highly developed infrastructure, which makes it a favoured destination among Americans. Many choose to settle here and establish their own businesses, moving their lives entirely from mainland USA. Costa Rica has a high literacy rate (more than 90%) thanks to its free and compulsory education system. Due to this developed structure and growing tourism, you will not be short of great places to stay.

There is a huge variety of accommodation to choose from. The best option is to go for one of the luxury beach lodges or an environmentally friendly mountain retreat. It is more than likely that your hotel will be run and managed by local people, who will know the area like the back of their hand. A basic grasp of Spanish will help to get the most out of your experience, so take a phrase book.

Overall, there are so many areas and places of interest in Costa Rica, especially for the cultural traveller, the nature enthusiast, and for the action adventure seeker.

 Fast Facts

Capital: San José

Location: Situated in the Central American isthmus, immediately north of Panama and bordering both the Caribbean Sea and the Pacific Ocean.

Population: 4,133,884.

Religion: 75% Roman Catholic, 14% Protestant, 11% other.

Languages: Spanish, English.

Opposite page, top. Tabacon Hot Springs.
Centre. Topiary trees in Sarchi.
Bottom. Coconuts in Tortugero.

Getting there and exploring around

Unfortunately, there are no direct flights to San José from the UK. However, there are many frequent flights from most major airports in the USA and South American. As such, you should expect to make a stopover in the USA if you are flying from the UK. The major airlines which fly to Costa Rica are American Airlines, Continental, United Airlines and Lacsa (which is the only airline that flies to all capitals in Central America).

Once you've arrived in Costa Rica, the best way to get around is by car. The public transport system can be very slow and the roads are not great. The Pan American - one of the main roads leading up to Arenal from San José Highway - is little more than a gravel path. Hiring a car is very easy, the airport has several internationally recognised car hire companies, and cars can be pre-booked online (advised during high season) or can be ordered upon arrival. It is worth noting that if you arrive late in the evening, some car hire places might be closed. In this instance it may be better to spend your first night near the airport so that you can collect you car in the morning and travel to your destination by daylight.

You can always opt for the 'Airpass Costa Rica', which gives you unlimited air travel to all destinations for one or two weeks with Sansa Airways. The airline flies regionally to main destinations around Costa Rica (from Tortuguero to Tamarindo). A one week air pass is $299 making it an economic and convenient way to get around Costa Rica.

Best time of year to visit

The early months of the rainy season (May to July) are a wonderful time to visit Costa Rica. Some towns experience a mini 'high season' during this time, namely Arenal and Punta Islita, despite the fact that rivers become swollen and dirt roads get muddy.

It's best to avoid the school holidays in June and July as prices can go through the roof. December is a very lively time of year for Christmas celebrations.

For surfers, the Pacific coast sees increased swells and bigger, faster waves during the wet season, peaking in the most rainy months of September and October. The Caribbean side has better waves from November through May. Divers may wish to plan their trip around high visibility seasons. The peak season for leatherback turtles is from April to May and for green turtles it's during August and September.

? Must know before you go

Etiquette. Keep your bathing suit on for the beach, don't strip off and dress modestly when walking around main towns. If you don't want to offend avoid saying 'no' just say 'gracias' instead - the locals don't say no to anything!

Buy local. Costa Rican coffee is a much 'fairer price' at local supermarkets than at the airport. Better still, if you are planning on taking a coffee tour at one of the plantations, buy at the local shop to help the local trade.

Must take. Pack a pair of good walking shoes for rambling around the national parks and exploring the volcanic regions. You'll also need some strong bug spray to ward off the aggressive mosquitoes, especially during the rainy season.

Highlights

San José. San José offers a wonderful mixture of traditional and modern architecture, great parks, markets, museums and informative coffee tours. Spend a few days here to get to know the history of Costa Rica.

San Lucas Island and Isla Del Coco. These islands have wonderful beaches and hidden pirates treasure. They also constitute a surfer's paradise with some of the best surfing in the world. The breaks are strong and consistent and attract surfers from all over the globe.

Arenal. This volcanic region has wonderful scenery and plenty of outdoor adventures. There are daily eruptions of red hot lava, waterfalls to swim in and natural hot outdoor springs for bathing and relaxing.

Tortuguero National Park. This national park is one of the most visited national parks in Costa Rica. Its network of canals, dense rainforests and lagoons hold a wealth of plant life and wildlife, especially turtles.

Adventure: Culture Vulture
Destination: San José

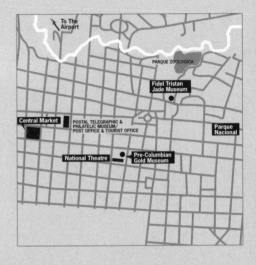

⊹ Regional Information

At first glance San José looks like a chaotic and raucous city. However, on closer inspection it is an inspiring and safe place with plenty of attractions to keep you busy, both in the city and just outside. For art enthusiasts, there is a handful of galleries and museums which display gold and jade artefacts. The pre-Columbian Gold Museum is run by state-owned Banco Central. There are more than 2,000 impressive pre-Columbian artefacts on display at this museum, including a collection of old coins in a nearby room. The pre-Columbian era incorporates all period subdivisions in the history and prehistory of the Americas before the appearance of significant European influences on the American continents. You will need to bring ID with you to the musuem as they won't let you in without it. An informative audio guide is also available if you want to learn more.

If you want to buy some souvenirs, Central Market is the place to go. The market is colourful and is set in an atmospheric setting. Traders sells good quality hand-made crafts, as well as baskets, flowers, spices, and hammocks. There are also booths selling many varieties of fish and meat, from octopus to pigs' heads. Furthermore, you can also find herbal remedies that claim to be able to cure everything! Just one word of warning about the market - pickpockets thrive in this area, so keep a watchful eye.

Opposite page. Clockwise from top.
Numberplate. Central Park, San José.
Café Britt tour. Coffee beans.

Costa Rica 21

Adventure: Culture Vulture
Destination: San José

Zoo Avenue is another of San José's must-see highlights. It is a sanctuary for injured animals, unusual wildlife and is a bird's paradise. It is located just outside the city centre and covers 59 hectares of landscaped gardens. The fantastic bird collection (the largest in Central America) includes dozens of toucans, cranes, curassows and parrots, and more than 100 other Costa Rican species of birds. Animal lovers will like the colourful macaws, deer and monkeys. There is also a relatively large crocodile! This place is excellent for families and anyone else who enjoys wildlife or wandering around landscaped gardens.

Café Britt Farm (20 minutes outside of San José) is one of the best coffee producers in Costa Rica. The company which owns the farm runs an extremely informative tour of every aspect of the farm - from planting to roasting. The company sells its coffee to speciality stores around the world and visitors can look at the coffee fields and sample the end product. There are five different tours to choose from. The standard 'Coffee Tour' takes you through the history of coffee making. Other tours take you through the butterfly gardens and the rainforest. All the tours conclude with a tasting session where you are shown how the experts taste coffee.

When the sun has set and you feel you still have some energy, San José has a wonderful nightlife scene. Downtown San José is very compact so you can get pretty much anywhere you want to go on foot. There are discos, dance clubs and plenty of bars in San José. Many of these will draw you to the dance floor with an intoxicating salsa beat. Just south of the University is a two-block stretch called La Calle de Amargure (Street of Bitterness). While the name doesn't sound inviting, it is a haven for the suburbanites and students, and contains a mix of bars and cafes with shops and bookstores.

If you're feeling a little more artsy then San José has a great selection of theatre and performing arts sessions. Burlesque, modern dance, theatre, symphony orchestras and classical concerts all vie for your attention. Every March, the country hosts El Festival Nacional de las Artes where you will have an amazing selection of things to choose from each night. For an up-to-date review on what's happening pick up a copy of Tico Times.

Before you head out though, a word of wisdom - street crime is a bit of a problem, so be careful and hang on to your purse.

Stylish Places to Stay

Natural Style: Alta Boutique Hotel. This stylish hotel has incredible views of the city below. The penthouse suite even has its own dining area and Moroccan fountain patio. Alta also features a wonderful glass-tiled pool, jacuzzi and gymnasium.

City Style: Costa Rica Marriott Hotel. Don't be put off by the fact that this hotel is part of chain. It is a gorgeous and authentic Costa Rican hotel. Rooms are all equipped with TVs, luxurious bathrooms and beautiful bed linen for a cosy night's sleep.

Chic Style: Xandari Resort and Spa. Located 25 km out of San José, this hotel is worth the trek if you want to relax away from the hustle and bustle but still be near enough to the city to enjoy its highlights.

Delicious Places to Eat

Rustic Charm: Bakea. This restored mansion has six dining rooms, a lovely bistro, a coffee house and terrace, and is perfect for evening dinners and lunchtime treats.

Typical Costa Rican: Mirador Ram Lunar. Try out this restaurant - it's a favourite with the locals. A popular dish is the Lomito Mirador which is beef tenderloin served with three savoury sauces. Wash it down with a local red. Wednesday night is an all-inclusive buffet with live music.

Peruvian Cuisine: Bohemia. Situated 500 metres from the church of Santa Teresita, this elegant restaurant is housed in an old restored mansion and presents authentic Peruvian dishes.

Top left. Pool at Xandari resort.
Top right. Costa Rican fiesta food.

Adventure: Nature Lover
Destination: Nicoya Peninsula

✦ Regional Information

Every visitor to Costa Rica sets their sights on the Nicoya Peninsula, known globally for its white sandy beaches and picture-postcard scenery. In particular, surfers and divers flock to this location because of its wonderful stretches of water and incredible offshore diving.

The Murcielagos Islands, Playa Grande and Ostional are excellent sites for marine turtles. The Pacific shore is the most interesting. It has various attractions, including the nation's first wildlife reserve. The choice of accommodation is growing quickly and you can find a great selection of quaint little B&B's and up-market resorts. To make the most of the peninsula's attractions you will need a couple of weeks. The area is vast and there is a lot to see, not just for nature enthusiasts, but also for beach and water sports fans.

Lying north of the peninsular, the Isla Murciélagos rises from the sea. Protected within the Santa Rosa National Park, the surrounding sea is renowned among divers and swimmers because of a huge range of marine life, from giant grouper and eagle rays to great bull sharks. Those who love marine life will thrive on a couple of days' stay here. There are several dive operators that offer diving safaris and day trips as well as snorkelling and sports fishing.

Red eyed green frog. Courtesy of
Getty Images.

Adventure: Nature Lover
Destination: Nicoya Peninsula

Situated further down the coastline, beaches don't come more natural and more beautiful than Playa Grande. The beach leads north through dry forests before ending at Playa Ventanas (suitable for snorkelling and bathing). The coral varies from coral-white to grey. Surfing experts highly rate this area. The hamlet of Comunidad Playa Grande is also on the main approach road, 600 metres inland from the beach, and is a lovely spot to stop by for lunch. The entire shoreline is protected within the 445-hectare Playa Grande Marine Turtle National Park (Parque Nacional Marino las Baulas), which guards the prime nesting site of the leatherback turtle on the Pacific coast, including 22,000 hectares out to sea. After a 15 year battle between developers and conservationists the beach was incorporated into the national park system in May 1990. The fate of the leatherback turtle was the central issue of debate. The beach also sweeps south to the mouth of the Matapalo river, which forms an estuary as it meets the sea. The estuary and its surrounding ecosystem are protected within the Tamarindo National Wildlife Refuge, and feature crocodiles, anteaters and monkeys, deer and ocelots.

Mal País is immediately north of Cabo Blanco and is a lively surfers' paradise, with some of the most incredible surfing in the country. A road that leads 10 km west from Cóbano hits the shore at the hamlet of Carmen, known in the surfing realm as Mal País. The tiny fishing hamlet of Mal País is actually 3 km south of Carmen. This dirt road dead-ends at the hamlet and turns inland briefly, ending at the northern entrance gate to Cabo Blanco Absolute Wildlife Reserve (entry to the park is not allowed here). A rocky track that begins 800 meters north of the dead-end links Cabuya with Mal País.

Isla Tortuga is a stunning 320 hectare island which lies 3 km offshore of Curú. Tortuga is as close to an idyllic tropical isle as you'll find in Costa Rica. The journey is about 90 minutes and there are several cruise companies which offer day trips to various sections of the island's beach. If you fancy something more active, there is a wonderful hike into the forested hills, where you can take a treetop canopy tour using professional climbing gear. Contact Calypso Cruises (on the Stylish Essentials page) for more information.

Cabo Blanco Absolute Wildlife Reserve is a jewel of nature perfect for nature enthusiasts. The reserve covers 1,172 hectares and is the oldest and most protected area in the country. Swedish immigrant Nils Olof Wessberg created it in October 1963. He and his wife settled in the area in 1955, when this corner of the peninsula was covered with a mix of evergreen and deciduous forest at a time when the area was becoming an area of rapidly falling trees, rising settlements and spreading cattle ranches. They bought a rocky, mountainous plot of land and spent 10 years developing fruit orchards. Olof was murdered in the Osa Peninsula in the summer of 1975 while campaigning to have the region declared a national park. A plaque near the Cabo Blanco ranger station stands in his honour. The reserve was originally off limits to visitors, but today about one third is accessible by hiking along the trails.

⤴ **Stylish Places to Stay**

Boutique Style: Casa Chameleon. This wonderful and very local place near Mal Pais is a great spot to explore the region. If you like intimate luxury with informal service then this is the place to stay.

Secluded Style: Punta Islita near Coyote. Offering gorgeous accommodation, from deluxe villas to suites, this place has an idyllic setting with views of the Pacific Ocean. They also have a zipline through the forest for those with an adventurous spirit. ★

Traditional Style: Cala Luna near Tamarindo. This hotel is set on the beach and is constructed from locally farmed tropical wood in a traditional style. It offers adventure and nature activities and is an enjoyable place to get away from it all.

🍴 Delicious Places to Eat

Homely Delights: Buenos Aires. This restaurant serves homemade food in a lovely setting and offers fresh fish everyday. It is integrated into the Hotel Buenos Aires near Mal Pais.

Jungle-sea Style: Nectar. This open-air restaurant serves creative local cuisine and international delights. Try the exquisite sushi and very fresh coffee (but not together). Situated in Florblanca Hotel, near Santa Teresa.

Al fresco Pizzas: Stella's. There is a large Italian population in Tamarindo and this is one of the city's best-rated restaurants. They serve good Italian pasta and fresh fish cooked in delicious and unusual sauces. There is even a wood-fired pizza oven for that true Italian flavour.

Top. Casa Chameleon. **Bottom.** Gazebo at Nectar.

Opposite page. Clockwise from top left.
Hanging bridge walk, Soak in hot springs,
Aerial runway.

Adventure: Action Hero
Destination: Arenal

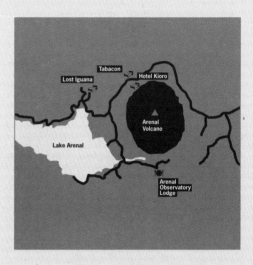

✦ Regional Information

Possibly the best area to explore if you are looking for adventure thrills is the volcanic Arenal. The active volcano that towers over the valley can be seen from miles away on a clear day. If you are lucky, on a clear night you can also see volcanic lava streaming out from its giant crater. This volcano has erupted every day since 1968 with each eruption lasting between two and 45 minutes. You can walk around the base of the volcano and be close enough to hear rocks falling and lava hissing. The national park advise you not to ascend higher than where the vegetation ends. Around the area, there are many activities, from rope bridge walks to aerial runways of 200 ft and higher (SkyTram and SkyTrek). Companies also offer waterfall rappelling (abseiling down tumbling waterfalls). These are excellent fun but are not for the faint-hearted.

One particular company (Pure Trek Adventures) offers a unique half-day rappelling adventure, which includes transport, rappelling and lunch. The journey alone up to the waterfalls is as exhilarating as the abseiling itself. The company usually accepts small groups and couples and it is a good way to meet like-minded travellers.

Other sights in the area include La Fortuna Waterfall, a 200 ft spectacle of cascading fresh rainforest water. The waterfall is located about 5.5 km outside of the town of La Fortuna. The steep climb down to the waterfall is through lush forests and rockery pools. You can swim and walk around the base of the waterfall, although a superb way to access the waterfalls is by horseback, which can be done as a morning or afternoon tour. After a long day exploring the many exciting activities, an excellent way to unwind is to soak yourself in one of the natural hot outdoor springs at Tabacon (there is also a hotel attached). This is enjoyed by both locals and tourists and has a great vibe. The pools are heated by the volcano but each pool varies in temperature; some are very hot and steamy while others are much cooler. There is also a great swim-up bar in the middle of the main pool where you can order drinks whilst soaking.

⌐ Stylish Places to Stay

Local Style: The Lost Iguana. The newly opened Lost Iguana Resort is an independently run hotel with beautifully designed interiors. Each room has a view of the volcano and a bath on the balcony, which makes it quite unique. Just remember to use some bug spray if you intend to bathe during the twilight hours, as the mosquitoes will attack. The hotel also has a small outdoor swimming pool and an excellent restaurant serving local and international cuisine.☆

Chic Style: Tabacon Resort. Recommended as the up-market resort in the area with plenty of facilities to keep you busy. They have wonderful hot springs where you can bathe at different temperatures from hot to moderate. There is also a fantastic swim up bar with local music to keep you entertained.

Minimalist Style: Arenal Kioro Suites & Spa. Newly opened and full of character, this place is a great hideaway. With direct views of the volcano and a gym in case you fancy a workout!

🍽 Delicious Places to Eat

Food with a view: Gingerbread. This pretty boutique hotel was newly opened in August 2006. It has a delightful setting and great views over the lake. A handful of dishes are on offer each day, and the menu depends entirely on the availability of fresh ingredients.

View of the Volcano: Arenal Observatory lodge. You can't get closer to the Volcanic action than this. Watch the Arenal volcano spit and bubble while eating fresh local produce, including freshly caught fish from Lake Arenal.☆

Butterfly Buzz: Restaurant Tipico Neolatino. This restaurant offers typical Costa Rican and Peruvian cuisine with Nuevo Latino touches. There is also an unusual butterfly and orchid garden behind the restaurant which you can explore while letting your dinner go down.

Opposite page. Fortuna waterfall.
This page. Top left. Lost Iguana Bedroom.
Top right. View of volcano from Arenal Observatory Lodge.

Focus On...
Tortuguero National Park

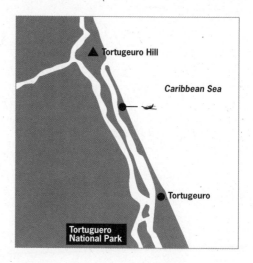

Tortuguero National Park is a 'must see' while in Costa Rica. Tortuguero National Park is located just south of the village Tortuguero. Accessible either by boat or plane, this small community has gradually developed as a direct result of green turtles' annual nesting process. In fact, this region is the most important nesting site in the entire western half of the Caribbean for the green turtle.

The park stretches north along the Caribbean coast up to the village of Tortuguero, which has a small population of around 500, no cars, and is located on a relatively narrow spit of land between the beach and a canal. Just north of Tortuguero are the various lodges and hotels. All these sections consist of a canal running parallel to the beach on the east, and are fed by a maze of serpentine streams and channels from the west.

The main reason to visit this area is to see the turtles nesting. From February to October, several species lay their eggs here. The park is the most important hatchery in the western Caribbean for Green sea turtles, but 3 other species also nest at Tortuguero - the Hawksbill, the Loggerhead, and the Giant Leatherback.

There are several other things to do here as well. Take a boat tour along the canals of the national park and beyond. Walk along the pristine beach. Visit the simple Tortuguero village and the Caribbean Conservation Corporation's visitor center and turtle museum. If energetic, climb the only hill in the area, the short but steep 150m high Cerro Tortuguero, for a great scenic view of the canals and ocean. (But beware of a fer de lance (snake) which sometimes lies on the path uphill - apparently the local guides know about it). The canals around the national park, and the ocean, also provide good fishing. We recommend at least 2 nights, preferably 3, to explore this area.

Opposite page. Turtle nesting in the national park. Courtesy of Getty Images.

(i) Stylish Essentials

General Information
www.govisitcostarica.com
www.visitcostarica.com

Continental Airlines
www.continental.com
T. 0845 6076760 (UK reservations)

Taca Airlines
www.taca.com
T. 08702 410 340 9 (UK reservations)

Sansa Airways
www.flysansa.com
T. +506 223 4179 (regional sales)

Avis Car Hire
www.avis.com

Tico Times
www.ticotimes.net

San José

The Museo del Oro pre-Columbino
www.museooro@racsa.co.cr
T. +506/243-4202
F. +506/243-4220
Open: 10.00 am – 4.30 pm
Tues–Sun. and holidays

Zoo Avenue
www.zooave.org
T. +506 433-8989
E. mailto:zooave@racsa.co.cr
F. +506/433-9140
Open: 9.00 am – 5.00 pm.
$9 admission adults, $4 children

Café Britt
Apdo. 528-3000, Heredia,
www. www.coffeetour.com
T. +506 260-2748
E. info@cafebritt.com
F. +506 238-1846

Mercado Central
Located between Avenidas Central/1
and Calles 6/8
Open: Every day, except Sunday.

Alta Boutique Hotel
www.thealtahotel.com
T. +506 282 4160

Costa Rica Marriott
www.marriott.com
T. +506 298 0000

Xandari Resort & Spa
www.xandari.com
T. +506 443 20202

Restaurant Bakea
www.restaurantbakea.com
T. +506 221 1051

Mirador Ram Lunar
T. +506 230 3060

Bohemia San José
AR 50017 Costa Rica
T. +506 253 6348
T. +506 230 3060

Nicoya Peninsular Region

El Ocotal Diving Safaris
www.ocotaldiving.com
Offers a free introductory dive daily
and rents equipment. It charges from
$64 for two-tank dives; night dives
cost $49. Snorkeling costs from
$25, full-day. Deep-sea fishing costs
$425/645 half-/full-day (up to four
people). Sportsfishing excursions are
also offered

Calypso Cruises
www.calypsocruises.com
T. +506 256-2727
F. +506 256-6767

**Refugio Nacional de Vida
Silvestre Tamarindo**
T. +506/296-7074

Cabo Blanco Absolute Wildlife
T. +506 642 0093 The ranger station
E. cablanco@ns.minae.go.cr
Camping is not allowed, even at the
ranger station.
Open: 8.00 am – 4.00 pm. Wed–Sun.
plus Monday and Tuesday during
holidays, $8 admission

Mal Pais Information
www.malpais.net

Florblanca Resort
www.florblanca.com
T. +506 640 0232

Casa Chameleon
www.hotelcasachameleon.com

Punta Islita
www.hotelpuntaislita.com
T. +506 231 6122

Cala Luna
www.calaluna.com
T. +506 653 0214

Buenos Aires Restaurant
www.buenosairesmalpais.com
T. +506 640 0254

Nectar Restaurant
(See Florblanca Resort)

Stella's Restaurant
www.stella.cr.com
T. +506 653 0127
Open: 7 days a week opening at
11.30 am

Arenal

**Canyoning Waterfall Rappelling
Company Pure Trek Adventures**
www.puretrekcostarica.com
T. +506 461 2110

Horseback Riding in Arenal
E. horsebackriding@arenal.com

Tabacon Springs & Resort
www.tabacon.com
T. +506 519 1900

SkyTram/SkyTrek
www.skytrek.com/english/arenal.html
T. +506 479 9944

Lost Iguana Resort
www.lostiguanaresort.com
T. +506 461 0122

Tabacon Resort
www.tabacon.com
T. +506 519 1900

Arenal Kioro Suites & Spa
www.hotelarenalkioro.com
T. +506 461 1700

Gingerbread
www.gingerbreadarenal.com
T. +506 694 0039
Open: 5.00 pm to 10.00 pm, Tuesday
to Saturday.

Arenal Observatory Lodge
www.arenalobservatorylodge.com
T. +506 290 7011

Restaurant Tipico Neolatino
T. +506 479 9186
Open: Daily 10.00 am-midnight

Tortuguero

General Information
www.tortugueroinfo.com

Underwater Belize. Courtesy of Getty Images

BELIZE

Belize City | Ambergris | Cayo District |
Lighthouse Reef

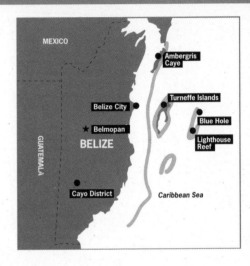

🏆 Why is this place so special?

Belize has become world renowned for its excellent dive sites, beaches and stylish accommodation. More recently, it has become a popular honeymoon destination. Situated in the very middle of Central America's East coast, Belize is an appealing country for travellers. It is easy to get around and is the only country in Central America where the official language is English.

Belize is bounded to the north by Mexico, to the south and west by Guatemala, and to the east by the Caribbean Sea with a coastline which is 174 miles long. Formerly know as British Honduras, it was colonised by the British Empire for more than a century, until it became fully independent in 1981. Prime Minister Said Musa, in power since 1998, has overseen the transformation of Belize's economy. Service industries, especially tourism, dominate where farming (logging and fishing) were once predominant.

Although Belize relies heavily upon tourism to sustain its economy, it also exports sugar, bananas and citrus fruits. Americans descend on Belize for long weekends and a few even have second homes there - as it is a relatively affordable and easy place to reach. Thankfully, however, this place is not full of fast food restaurants and there are none of the chains you might see littering the USA. Instead, there are local eateries and street vendors selling tamales - chicken wrapped in plantain leaves - as well as exotic traditional food such as armadillo.

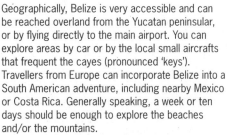

Geographically, Belize is very accessible and can be reached overland from the Yucatan peninsular, or by flying directly to the main airport. You can explore areas by car or by the local small aircrafts that frequent the cayes (pronounced 'keys'). Travellers from Europe can incorporate Belize into a South American adventure, including nearby Mexico or Costa Rica. Generally speaking, a week or ten days should be enough to explore the beaches and/or the mountains.

Ambergris Caye is the most popular destination among backpackers, divers and American tour groups. Recently, there has been an increase in new luxury lodges. The lovely beaches and water sports make this a superb destination for the 'fly and flop' type traveller.

That said, there is plenty to see around Belize if you're willing to stray away from the other tourists. If you venture out of the centre, Belize City has an air of colonial charm with some interesting art museums and Mayan ruins. The Cayo District is great for those who love scenery and wildlife. It boasts a huge cave system, two of Belize's most important Mayan ruins, and forests rich with wildlife. Belize is very much 'on the map' as a must-see destination in Central America.

📷 Fast Facts

Capital: Belmopan

Location: Situated on the east coast of Central America on the Caribbean Sea, Belize is bordered by Guatemala to the south and west, by Mexico to the north.

Population: 287,730.

Religion: 49.6% Roman Catholic, 27% Protestant, 23.4% other.

Language: English, Spanish, Crioulo, Garifuna.

Getting there and exploring around

Belize City has two airports: Philip Goldson International Airport (BZE) which is 18 km (11 miles) north west of the city centre; and the Municipal Airstrip (TZA), which is around 3 km (2 miles) north of the city centre. While international flights only use the international airport, domestic flights use both - flights using the Municipal Airstrip are always cheaper.

The Caye Caulker Water Taxi Association is the main service connecting Belize City with Caye Caulker (1 hr) and San Pedro (Ambergris Caye, 1.5 hrs). On request, boats will stop at Long Caye or Caye Chapel. The Thunderbolt departs for Caye Caulker and San Pedro from its dock at North Front St, west of the Swing Bridge. Alternatively, if you want to get to Ambergris Caye quicker there are short flights that leave Philip Goldson Airport but stop off briefly at the Municipal airport. The flights are quick but it can be a bumpy and nervy ride if you are not used to low-level flying (see Stylish Essentials for more details).

The main bus services from and to Belize City are run by Novelo's bus line (see Stylish Essentials for more details). The terminal in Belize City is a run-down area so you should get a taxi there. Express services are more expensive, but they are quicker and usually more comfortable than regular ones. Take a first-class ticket rather than an economy one. Destinations include Belmopan, Benque Viejo del Carmen, Chetumal, Mexico, Corozal, Dangriga, Maskall, Orange Walk, Punta Gorda and San Ignacio.

If you want to brave the roads you can hire a car. The main road in and out of Belize City is the Northern Highway. It heads north west from the Belcan Junction and the Western Highway - the Westward continuation of Cemetery Road. Car hire companies are concentrated around the main city and airport, so do your research to find the most practical way to get there.

Best time of year to visit

Belize it is relatively hot and humid throughout the year, although the dry season (November to May) is less humid with clearer skies - perfect conditions for sightseeing and walking. This time of year is also the busiest for tourists.

Still, many visitors prefer the quieter days of the rainy season - from June to October. During this time, the weather is much more tropical and short downpours are frequent, but hotel rates are lower during this time, which is good for those wanting to save a bit of cash. Both times of the year have their own unique attractions, and the choice of when to visit is totally up to you, your budget and the adventure you crave. We recommend that check out the local conditions before you fly. If you are planning a trip based around good weather you can make changes to a trip if necessary or plan something different.

? Must know before you go

Insect repellent. This is an absolute essential, especially when visiting the cayes. The local mosquitoes are lethal and will leave huge nasty bites if you are not careful. It is a good idea is to buy after-sun with added insect repellent or, if you don't like the smell of DEET, citronella spray.
Sampling the local cuisine. Take your time to experience the local cuisine with Caribbean and Latin American flavours. Locally grown and prepared food is abundant, healthy, easy to find and quite affordable.
Keep your wits about you. Theft is ubiquitous in Belize and you should be very cautious about your personal belongings around Belize City. Ambergris Caye is another area where you should be careful, especially if you have hired a golf buggy (ours was actually stolen!)

Highlights

Belize City. Arts and museum buffs will love exploring Belize City, the cultural heart of Belize. The historical Fort George and the Altun Ha ruins are must-see attractions.
Ambergris Caye. There are wonderful local lodges and swish spas to indulge your senses at Ambergris Caye. Just right for beach lovers and those seeking a relaxing getaway!
Cayo District. Wildlife, lush forests, stunning scenery and magnificent Mayan temples await you at Cayo District - it's a wonderful area for exploring the great outdoors.
Blue Hole Diving. The Blue Hole is an incredible dive site and noted as being one of the best in the world (see Focus On... Diving the Blue Hole on page 57).

Top left. Underwater garden reefs.
Bottom left. Mayan temples in Cayo District (El Castillo).

Adventure: Culture Vulture
Destination: Belize City & District

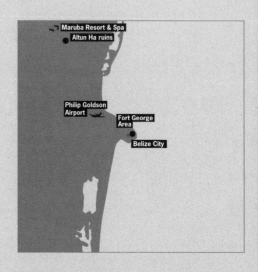

Regional Information

Initially, Belize City's urban scenery doesn't have the appeal of most other Central American cities. However, if you ignore the stinking canals and scruffy slums, the city offers some striking colonial houses, seaside parks and bustling shopping areas as well as some cute sailboats at the mouth of Haulover Creek. Exploring the city's streets can be very hot during the summer, occasionally threatening, but rarely dull. A couple of days is usually enough to explore the city and its surrounding areas.

Belize City is no longer the political capital of the country, although it is still home to a quarter of its population. It is a haven for creative minds and boasts the best of Belizean arts, entertainment, shops and restaurants. It is also the perfect base to explore the country's stunning ancient and natural wonders.

If you are interested in the history of Belize then the Museum of Belize, based in Gabourel Lane, is a must-see. It is housed in the country's former main prison, which was built in 1857, and even one of the original cells is preserved in its original state, complete with inmates' graffiti. The museum contains photos and documents of the country's colonial era as well as material on national disasters, such as hurricanes. Sadly, most of Belize's finest Mayan treasures are in other countries, so the Mayan Treasures area is a little poor, but there are still some interesting sculptures on show.

For art buffs, Belize has an exciting and emerging art scene, starting at The Image Factory Shop and Gallery. In addition to browsing, you can learn about concerts and cultural events in the city. Also, visit the Fine Arts Gallery on Front Street then skip to Southside and walk by the Bliss Institute and Government House/House of Culture just down the seawall.

Opposite page. Top. Transport around Belize. **Bottom.** Altun Ha ruins.

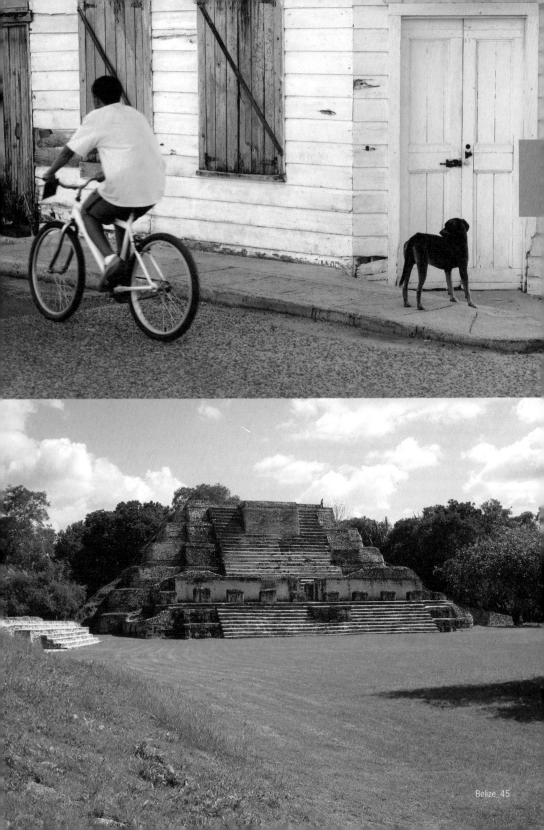

Adventure: Culture Vulture
Destination: Belize City
& District

The central focus of Belize City life is the Swing Bridge, built in 1923 and a product of Liverpool's ironworks. Connecting Belize City's north and south sides, the Swing Bridge is the only manually operated swing bridge still functioning in the world. It is swung every morning and evening to allow boats to pass through the river. Interestingly, the operators of the bridge sometimes rope in bystanders to help turn the cranks.

One of the most pleasant areas in Belize City is Fort George. Wander around the neighbourhood and you'll pass some lovely homes. A few of them have become charming old guesthouses. The Baron Bliss Memorial and the Fort George Lighthouse stand guard over the old, stately upscale hotels, embassies and restaurants. This is a wonderful location for an evening stroll.

Until the 1850s, Fort George dock and Fort George Island belonged to the Army as a barracks. After World War II, visiting dignitaries from England surveyed the country, armed with plans for various agricultural projects to help the people, but they couldn't find a place to stay. So accommodation went to the top of their list and this became one of the first post-war projects in the colony. An easy-going, low-key charmer with excellent service and tasty meals, Fort George became the best hotel in town. Today, the hotel is part of the Radisson chain and has taken over the Villa Hotel across the street, one block off the waterfront.

If you want to escape Belize City for the day, then the Altun Ha Ruins are not to be missed. Altun Ha was a Mayan trading centre as well as a religious ceremonial centre and is believed to have once accommodated as many as 10,000 people. The construction of the temple is thought to date back 1,500 - 2,000 years. The Mayan name Altun Ha literally means 'Rockstone Pond' and was coined when archeologists (lead by a team from the Royal Ontario Museum) arrived in 1964. The team uncovered many valuable finds, such as unusual green obsidian blades, pearls, and more than 300 jade pieces, beads, earrings and rings. Seven funeral chambers were discovered, including the Temple of the Green Tomb, which was rich with human remains and traditional funerary treasures. A solid jade head was also found, which is now referred to as Kinich Ahau (The Sun God) and is believed to be the largest jade carving found in any of the Mayan countries.

The Altun Ha ruins have become one of the most popular day-trips for groups and independent travellers from Belize City, so if you want to beat the crowds, try and get there before everyone else, or stay locally the night before. If you want to give something back to the community, hire a local tour guide and buy some local crafts from one of the many sellers.

↘ Stylish Places to Stay

Sea front style: Radisson Fort George Hotel.
A convenient location close to the cultural and commercial attractions of Belize City makes this place a good choice for those wanting to explore. Rooms which overlook the Caribbean Sea are the best. This is a full-service resort with pool, fitness facilities and restaurants.

Colonial Style: The Great House, Belize City.
Winner of Best Boutique Hotel 2004 by *Caribbean Travel and Life Magazine*, this place has colonial charm and a simple but gorgeous courtyard restaurant. The rooms all have polished pine floors and simple decorations. Fresh fruit is normally served on arrival.

Jungle Style: Maruba Resort and Spa. North of the Altun Ha ruins, this 'tribal chic' resort has a real getaway feel. They have a gorgeous outdoor pool and a Japanese hot tub to soak your weary feet after a long day trekking around the sights. ★

◉ Delicious Places to Eat

Burger and Beers: Riverside Tavern. This tavern claims to have the best burger in Belize. It is owned by locals who brew Belikin beer (the local beer). The Tavern is quite new but is building up a loyal local client base, so it must be good.

Upmarket Style: The Smoky Mermaid. Located in a wonderful 1927 colonial home, just a few feet away from the Fort George dock, this place offers gorgeous Caribbean and International cuisine on a lovely patio with a typical Belizean reggae band usually playing onstage.

Travellers tavern: Jambel's Jerk Pit. This eatery offers local Belizean and Jamaican food, such as spicy curries, shrimp Creole, lobster and jerk chicken. There are about five tables in the main dining room, but your best bet is to grab one of the tables in the outdoor courtyard, a favourite among seasoned travellers.

Top left. Radisson Fort George.
Top right. Lobster food at the Smoky Mermaid.

Adventure: Beach Bum
Destination: Ambergris Caye

✦ Regional Information

Ambergris Caye is a popular getaway destination for those wanting a relaxed ambiance, stretches of beaches and the subtle hustle and bustle of a summer party scene.

Ambergris inspired Madonna's song 'La Isla Bonita', which means 'the beautiful island. It is the largest island in Belize and has become a popular destination with Americans who want a quick and easy weekend away. It offers good value for money and warm weather. As such, it's also a popular destination for honeymooners and couples. The excellent beaches, clear waters and fine reef make it a great place for diving, snorkelling, swimming, fishing and sailing.

San Pedro town is the only town on the island, so this is where you will land (on the very short airstrip) if you have taken a flight from Belize City. The town is laid back and there are waterfront bars and restaurants everywhere. There are very few cars, so the best way to get around is by hiring a golf buggy (but make sure you lock it up if you leave it anywhere - ours got stolen). Between the north part of Ambergris Caye and San Pedro there is a creek crossing (classed as a ferry) which is manually pulled by locals, a couple of golf carts, bikes and the occasional stray dog! You can buy tickets to cross the creek from the nearby hut.

Top right. Beach, Ambergris Caye.
Bottom right. Hand Ferry Crossing.

Adventure: Beach Bum
Destination: Ambergris Caye

Swimming and relaxing on the beach are the main activities at Ambergris Caye. All the beaches are public and most waterside hotels are fairly generous with their deck chairs. Water at the shore tends to be quite shallow, and most areas have heavy seagrass. A number of hotels remove the seagrass. While not a good move environmentally, this does make the swimming more pleasant. The best swimming areas are at Ramons village pier and Banana Beach resort. The further north or south you go, the less people there are and the more private the beaches become.

The views of the turquoise water and reefs from the beaches are spectacular, and at least when the offshore prevailing winds are blowing, which is most of the time, there are fewer mosquitoes. North Ambergris Caye has long stretches of beach that are tropically beautiful.

If you are looking for a short trip, there are several companies which offer manatee watching and Caye Culker tours by boat. The rocky point snorkel trip and barbeque is wonderful. Boats leave early to head north and stop off at Blue Point, Basil Jones and Mexico rocks (the main snorkel sites) and while you relax they cook up a barbeque on the beach. Popular tour companies include Amigos del Mar, Lady Sharon Sunset, Champagne Tours or Tanisha Ecotours. You can also snorkel off the beach at your hotel or anywhere on the island, but you're unlikely to see as much as you do on these trips.

The Hol Chan Marine Reserve is a bit of a haven for visitors. Situated on the south of the Caye, it can be visited by boat with one of the many dive operators. As many as 75,000 visitors visit Belize each year and Hol Chan is now one of the most popular dive and snorkel sites. Once you visit, you'll quickly understand why the reserve is so popular. Please remember that it's just as important to preserve it for future visitors (see Reef Etiquette Guidelines in 'Focus On...Diving the Blue Hole' on page 57 for more details).

This marine park was established in 1987 in order to preserve a small but complete section of the Belize Barrier Reef. Because of the no-fishing restrictions near the reef, the site boasts an amazing diversity of species. The reserve focuses its energy on creating a sustainable link between tourism and conservation, protecting the coral reef while allowing visitors to experience and learn about the beauty of the marine life living there.

Top right. Victoria House.
Bottom right. Mambo restaurant, Mata Chica.

↘ Stylish Places to Stay

Beachside Style: Blue Tang Inn. This beachside retreat on the north side of the town has a lovely private pool area, which makes you think you are a million miles away from the town of San Pedro. The best rooms are the deluxe ones which have vaulted ceilings and spa tubs.

Colonial Style: Victoria House. Beautiful colonial white house with a stunning beach, gardens and swimming pool. You can choose from a beachfront *casita* (little house) or a villa with infinity pool. Rooms are beautifully designed with handcrafted mahogany beds and walk-in showers. This luxury house is situated south of the town and they have their own dive shop on site.★

Sports Style: Villas at Banyan Bay. Further north, but not too far away, this is a great place for watersports enthusiasts. They have extensive grounds, a large swimming pool and a complete array of watersports - from kayaks to hobie cats and sailing boats. They can also arrange dive tours too.

🍽 Delicious Places to Eat

Local Boho Charm: Mambo restaurant at Mata Chica. Located away from the hustle and bustle of downtown San Pedro, this gorgeous place is decorated with pure boho charm entwined with a slightly Moroccan ethnic theme. If you are lucky enough to be visiting during the lobster season, it serves the best grilled lobster we have ever tasted. ★

Rooftop Dishes: Jambel Jerk Pit. With the only rooftop patio in town, this serves hot Jamaican dishes that can be spiced according to your intolerance. Brave the crazy hot dish if you dare!

Seaside Charm: Admiral Nelson's Barefront Beachfront Bar. Based at the Victoria House Hotel, this is a lovely café-style restaurant. The food is excellent and the service is attentive but not intrusive.

Adventure: Nature Lover
Destination: Cayo District

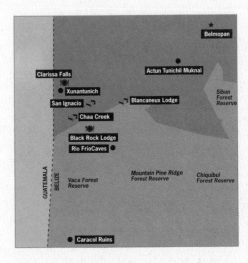

✦ Regional Information

The Cayo District is rapidly becoming one of the Belize's most popular destinations for
nature and wildlife lovers due to the expansive scenery and jungle trails. Most visitors
agree that although each area has its own charms, the Cayo District stands out head
and shoulders above the others. With an area of over 2,000 square miles, it is the
largest and the most diverse region of Belize. It is rich in history (the Caracol and
Xuanantunich Mayan ruins) and nature (with over 500 hundred species of birds). Cayo is
also home to one of the world's largest caving systems, as well as the refreshing heights
of the Mountain Pine Ridge.

The area, which borders Guatemala, offers hiking trails and lazy rivers which
can be toured on foot or horseback. The clean mountain water of the Pine Ridge awaits
you in dozens of caves, waterfalls, swimming holes - and maybe even a hot tub. To
experience this area it is a good idea to spend a week here, fully exploring the myriad
of caves, ruins, rivers and lush scenery.

The Mountain Pine Ridge area is south of San Ignacio and the Western Highway.
The sudden switch from tropical rainforest to pine trees as you ascend to the ridge is
fascinating. The reserve is full of rivers, pools, waterfalls and caves. Not to be missed
are the Rio Frio Caves, which are easily accessible and can be incorporated on the
Caracol and Mountain Ridge tour. The pools make a lovely spot for a picnic lunch.
To explore this area if you don't have a car, the best option is to use a local tour guide
from San Ignacio.

Adventure: Nature Lover
Destination: Cayo District

Beyond the Pine Ridge are the Caracol ruins, Belize's largest and most important Mayan site. Caracol was once the most powerful cities in the Mayan world, but now lies surrounded by jungle near the Guatamalan border - which is approximately a 2 hour drive from San Ignacio. Caracol is not only an archeological site of importance but is also an exciting jungle setting. Most visitors come on a guided tour, but like the Mountain Pine Ridge it is possible to hire a car and do it yourself. Overnight stays are not permitted so make sure you get up early to avoid the crowds.

Xunantunich is Belize's most accessible Mayan site. The name, according to one interpretation, means 'Maiden of the Rock' in the Yucateć dialect, and is pronounced 'zshoo-NAN-too-NEECH.' It was the first site in Belize to be opened to the public, when the road and a ferry were built in 1954. The tallest temple is the 130 ft 'El Castillo', which is large by Mayan standards and is only exceeded by the Caana pyramid at Caracol. The site was occupied until around 900 AD and was likely abandoned after an earthquake. You can climb to the top of El Castillo to enjoy a spectacular 360-degree view of the area. There is a good visitor centre which explains more about the history of the ruins and is located between the ticket office and the hilltop ruins.

Actun Tunichil Muknal is quickly becoming Belize's most popular underground experience. This cave is for fit and active people who do not mind getting wet and muddy and who are able to tread lightly. After the initial 45-minute hike to the entrance (with three river fords) and a swim into the cave's innards, you will be asked to remove your shoes to climb up the limestone into the main cathedral-like chambers. The rooms are littered with delicate Maya pottery and the crystallised remains of 14 humans. There are no pathways, fences, glass or other partitions separating the visitor from the artefacts. Nor are there any installed lights. The only infrastructure is a rickety ladder leading up to the chamber of the cave dwelling itself. A full female skeleton sparkles with calcite under your headlamp's glare. Only two tour companies are licensed to take guests here: Pacz Tours and Mayawalk, both based in downtown San Ignacio.

Medicinal Jungle Trail and Iguana Exhibit is an interpretative medicinal herb trail and iguana breeding project which is accessed through the San Ignacio Resort Hotel, on 14 riverside acres, and is well worth the visit. Tours of the herb trail or the iguana project are available for less than £4 per person - allow 45 minutes for either talk. With the money earned from tourists, the hotel owners are able to keep the trail maintained and the iguana project going. They are also able to prevent the heavily vegetated riverbank from being developed (crucial to the cleanliness of the local water supply). To date, 175 species of birds have been observed here (including a rare family pair of black hawk eagles). The medicinal trail takes you through the neighbouring forests and information is given on medicinal uses of Belizean plants complemented by on-site material. This is a wonderful experience for those who love nature.

⤳ Stylish Places to Stay

Swanky Style: Chaa Creek Resort. This is a newly refurbished and upgraded hotel with a newly hired chef who is winning rave reviews for combining classical Continental techniques with spices of the Caribbean. Located onsite is the famous butterfly farm, Chaa Creek national history museum, and the rainforest medicine trail.

Local Style: San Ignacio Resort Hotel. Located in San Igancio Town just 75 miles west of Belize City, this resort is perched above the lush Macal River Valley on 17 acres of land. Most of the 24 rooms have great views of rainforest, hillsides, and a pool, bringing the jungle and all its intrigue just steps away. They also offer guided tours to the Green Iguana Exhibit and to the Medicinal and Jungle Trails.

Indulgent Style: Blancaneaux Lodge. Originally an indulgent lodge set up as a private retreat for movie director Francis Ford Coppola, this place has its own stables, a hot pool, walking trails and riverside spa. Set in the Mountain Pine Ridge area, you can indulge and feast upon food from the lodge's own organic garden. ⭐

🍽 Delicious Places to Eat

Belizean Style: Clarissa Falls restaurant. Located in San Ignacio, this open-air restaurant, with a thatched roof sits atop the mound of a Mayan pyramid and beside the Mopan River. Drink homemade lemonade and feast upon typical Belizean dishes. They also have a wonderful vegetarian and vegan selection.

Fresh and fun: Black Rock Lodge restaurant. Set upon the Macal River this cute lodge offers some great local food, all hand-made, fresh and served on a long wooden table - so you can enjoy the company of other fellow travellers. It also has a hotel attached with deluxe cabanas.

Organic: Pine Ridge Lodge. This lodge is located near the Caracol ruins and produces some of its own organic homegrown food. There is no electricity here, but the restaurant still manages to cook up delicious meals using butane gas.

Top left. Blancaneux Lodge.
Top right. Black Rock Lodge.

Focus On...
Diving the Blue Hole in Lighthouse Reef

This justifies a special mention. Belize is home to one of the top dive sites in the world: the Blue Hole, a geographical phenomenon. The Blue Hole offers an incredible dive experience, not only for the reef formations, but also for the astonishing marine life. With sharks, trigger fish and tonnes of other reef fish, this place is a dream for those who love marine life.

The Blue Hole is a collapsed cavern of stalactites and stalagmites spreading a quarter of a mile across. In various places massive limestone stalactites hang down from what was once, before the end of the last Ice Age, a ceiling of air-filled caves. The circular shape is darker blue than the turquoise sea surrounding the area, and its depth is around 300 metres.

The dive site itself is serviced by two registered dive companies: Amergris Divers and Amigoes. This is a long day trip and usually has a very early start with a lunch stop on one of the local nature islands, and a second shallower dive in the afternoon.

The Blue Hole dive is recommended for experienced divers, with an advanced qualification and a minimum of 25 logged dives. The dive exceeds the recreational dive limit of 40 metres (actual dive depth is around 45 metres), so additional insurance and longer safety stops are strongly recommended.

Reef Etiquette Guidelines:

1. Do not touch the coral reef
2. Do not take anything from the sea
3. Do not chase or antagonise the marine life
4. If you see any litter pick it up and take it with you
5. By keeping your buoyancy neutral you can prevent unsettling the sea bed

Opposite page. Ariel view of Blue Hole.
Courtesy of Getty Images.

ⓘ Stylish Essentials

General Information
www.travelbelize.org

Airlines

Tropic Air
www.tropicair.com
T. +501 226 2012 (from Belize)
E. reservations@tropicair.com

Maya Air
www.mayaairways.com
T. +501 223 1140 (from Belize)
E. info@mayaisland.com

Car Hire
www.avis.com.bz

Diving Companies

Amigos del Mar Dive Shop
www.amigosdive@btl.net
T. +501-2-62706
F. +501 2-62648
This shop, on a pier near the center
of San Pedro Town

Blue Hole Dive Shop
www.bluehole@btl.net
T. +501 2-62982
F. +501 2-62981

Hustler Tours Pro Dive Shop
www.hustler@btl.net
T. +501 2-62279
F. +501 2-63468

Ramon's Village
www.ramons@btl.net
T. +501 2-62071
F. +501 2-62214

Belize City

Altun Ha Ruins Altun Ha
T. +501 609 3540
Open: 9.00 am – 5.00 pm,
Cost: US$3 per person

Museum Of Belize
www.museumofbelize.org
Open: Mon-Fri 9.00 am – 5.00 pm
Sat 9:00 am – 1.00 pm

**The Image Factory Shop
and Gallery**
www.imagefactory.bz/whoarewe.shtml

The Swing Bridge
www.travelbelize.org/bc.html

Radisson Fort George Hotel
www.radisson.com/belizecitybz
T. +501 223 3333

The Great House in Belize City
www.greathousebelize.com
T. +501 223 3400

Maruba Resort & Spa
www.maruba-spa.com
T. +501 225 5555

Riverside Tavern
North Front Street
T. +501 223 5640

Smokey Mermaid
13 Cork St
T. +501 223 4759

Jambel's Jerk Pit
2B King St
T. +501 227 6080

Ambergris Caye

Tanisha ecotours
www.tanishatours.com

Blue Tang Inn
www.bluetanginn.com
T. +501 226-2326

Victoria House
www.victoria-house.com
T. +501 226-2067

Villas at Banyan Bay
www.banyanbay.com
T. +501 226-3739

Mata Chica
www.matachica.com
T. +501 220 5010
Open: For dinner only

Jambel Jerk Pit
T. +501 226 3303
Open: All day dining

**Admiral Nelsons Barefront Beach-
front Bar (Victoria House)**
T. +501 226-2067
Open: Breakfast, lunch and dinner

Cayo District

General information and tours
www.belizex.com

Pacz Tours
www.pacztours.net/index.html

Mayawalk
www.mayawalk.com

Everalds Caracol Shuttle tours
T. +501 804 0090
E. caracolshuttle@hotmail.com
Caracol tours and Rio Frio Cave tours.

Chaa Creek
www.chaacreek.com
T. +501 824 2037

San Ignacio Resort Hotel
www.sanignaciobelize.com
T. +501 824 2034

Blancaneaux Lodge
www.blancaneauxlodge.com
T. +501 824 4912

Clarissa Falls
www.clarissafalls.com/clarissa-dining.
shtml
T. +501-9-23916
Open: Daily 7.00 am – 7.00 pm

Black rock Lodge Restaurant
www.blackrocklodge.com/restaurant.
html
T. +501-824-2529
Open: Daily

Pine Ridge Lodge
www.pineridgelodge.com
T. +501-606-4557
Open: Daily

Mexican Taxi

MEXICO

Mexico City | Los Cabos | Yucatán |
Bay of Banderas

MEXICO

Chihuahua

Gulf of Mexico

Los Cabos

Bay of Banderas

Mexico City

Yucatán

North Pacific Ocean

🏆 Why is this place so special?

Mexico exudes a charming mix of modern and traditional experiences, which is one of the reasons why travellers are so drawn to the country. Whether your passion is downing mojitos, listening to a *mariachi* (a Mexican musical eight-piece group), exploring Mayan ruins or celebrating 'The Day of the Dead', there is a vibe about Mexico that makes it a difficult place to leave.

Colour permeates from every aspect of Mexican life and it is this that makes the country so different to anywhere else in the world. The first thing to hit first time visitors to Mexico will be the colourful architecture, artists, textiles and food. Everything seems to display vibrant yellows, greens and reds.

Mexico has one of the largest tourism industries in the world. In 2005 it was the seventh most popular tourist destination worldwide - over 20 million tourists visit each year. The most notable attractions are ancient ruins and popular beach resorts. The coastal climate and unique culture - a fusion of Spanish and Meso-American cultures - also draw tourists. As Mexico is so immense and diverse, you will really need two or three weeks as a minimum. Many travellers end up extending their stay for longer.

Northern Mexico is renowned for its extreme weather, expansive deserts, nature reserves and rugged mountain ranges. This is in contrast to the culture of Central Mexico, where there are colonial cities, world heritage sites and fascinating museums.

Southern Mexico and the Gulf of Mexico feature an abundance of marshland, swamps and forests, which are ideal for outdoor adventure seekers and for those who love the natural environment.

The Yucatan Peninsula has some of Mexico's most famous temples, such as Chichen Itza and Tulum. Beach resorts, coral reefs and submerged caves make this a good overall destination for those wanting culture, scenery and a beach holiday all in one.

From top. Downtown Mexico city, Palm trees of Yucatan, Chichen Itza temple.

The Pacific Coast is perfect for culinary and gastronomic enthusiasts and has some of the best surfing and fishing. The Baja California Peninsula is an important feature of the Pacific Coast and is a getaway for wealthy Americans from California. The famous city of Cabo San Lucas, at the southern tip of the peninsula, entertains a host of golf lovers, sea enthusiasts and beach bums, as well as those seeking a glimpse of the incredible Grey Whale.

Mexico's historical attractions - such as the ancient ruins of the Olmecs, Mayas, and Aztecs - are a key reason why travellers come here.

The tale of Mexico's past, accompanied by an overwhelming collection of ancient ruins, is as romantic, dramatic and complex as it gets.

A luxury backpacker in Mexico will never be short of places to stay, including magnificently restored haciendas, hip hotels, beach lodges or skyscraper inns.

Fast Facts

Capital: Mexico City.

Location: Situated between the USA to the north and Belize and Guatemala to the south. Mexico also has coast lines with the Pacific to the west and the Gulf of Mexico to the east.

Population: 108,000,000.

Religion: 90% Roman Catholic, 7% Christian, 3% other.

Languages: Spanish, Nahutl.

Getting there and exploring around

Mexico's proximity to the USA, the Pacific Ocean and the Gulf of Mexico makes it a very accessible destination.

Getting to Mexico is easy. An abundance of international airlines service Mexico City and Cancun directly from the UK and from the USA. Around 30 Mexican cities receive direct flights from the USA and Canada, and there are plenty of cheap connections to the Caribbean and the rest of Latin America.

If travelling overland, travellers can cross into Mexico by road from the USA at one of the 40 official crossing points. Most cross-border bus services travel from Texas. There are 10 border crossings between Mexico and Guatemala, and fairly frequent bus services between border points and Guatemalan towns. Frequent buses also run between Belize City and Chetumal (you can hop on an executive coach for next to nothing and be entertained all the way). One company which provides an excellent tour service to Mexico from Belize is Gorge & Esther Moralez (see Stylish Essentials). They are reliable and have a lot of local knowledge.

Trains run from San Diego to Tijuana, El Paso to Ciudad Juárez, and Del Rio to Ciudad Acuña. The Great Rail Journeys (see Stylish Essentials) runs a 14 day tour around California, USA, and stops in Tijuana. If you want to explore in style this is the way to do it.

Hiring a car within Mexico is a good option and provides you with freedom and flexibility. A car also allows you to explore the immense countryside and escape from other tourists. Be advised, however, that local police can target foreigners and hire cars are easily spotted. If you happen to get pulled over be accommodating and don't try to be clever with the police.

Best time of year to visit

Mexico is enjoyable most of the year, but October to May is generally the most pleasant time to visit in terms of the climate. The May to September period can be hot and humid, particularly in the south.

The peak tourist seasons are during December and during July and August, with brief surges at many beach resorts during the week before Easter (Semana Santa) and during American colleges' spring break (March to April).

Mexico's climate has something for everyone: it's hot and humid along the coastal plains, and drier and more temperate at higher elevations inland (Guadalajara or Mexico City, for example).

Opposite page. From top. Colourful hacienda, making quesadillas, vibrant costumes in Tulum.

? Must know before you go

Learn the lingo. Learning a little Spanish before travelling can certainly help you get by. Communicating with the locals in their language is always appreciated, particularly in some of the more remote areas.

Driving and taxis. If you return to your parked car to find the front licence plate missing, you have been given a parking ticket - you get the plate back after paying the fine at the police station. Wave your forefinger (think 'no-no') if a cab or bus pulls up and you don't need a ride. Try to take cabs from authorised taxi stands as unlicensed cab drivers may charge outrageous fares.

Keep an open mind and go with the flow. Despite some of the threats and dangers in Mexico, learn to read a situation. One of the joys of travelling to a different country is seeing how things are done differently - in some cases these may seem positive and in other situations they may drive you up the wall. The important thing is to take it as a learning experience. Enjoy yourself and have a good time.

Crime. Despite all the hype about Mexico, it does have a problem with crime in some areas and travellers do need to be aware of the risks and dangers. Mexico City is known to be one of the most dangerous cities in the world. Most hotels, restaurants and shops have their own security guards and their own taxis, which are the best option if you don't want to get ripped off, or worse, mugged.

⚓ Highlights

Day of the Dead. The country's most characteristic and original fiesta is the wonderfully ghoulish Día de los Muertos, held the day after All Saints' Day on the 2nd of November. The souls of the dear departed are believed to return to earth on this day, and for weeks beforehand the country's markets are littered with the much-prized candy skulls, papier-mâché and skeletons.

Frida Kahlo Museum in Mexico City. This museum is dedicated to Frida Kahlo, an enigmatic artist famed for her work and social exploits. A visit to the museum, which is set in her former home and is filled with artworks and stories of her difficult life, makes a fascinating day out.

Beach of Cabo San Lucas. This beach stretches for miles and the sea is fierce and captivating. The Sea of Cortez meets the Pacific Ocean at the land's end point, making unusual colours in the water. This is a perfect spot for sun worshippers.

Mayan Temples. Explore the wonderful temples of Chichen Itza and Tulum whilst driving along the picturesque Yucatan peninsula.

Adventure: Culture Vulture
Destination: Mexico City

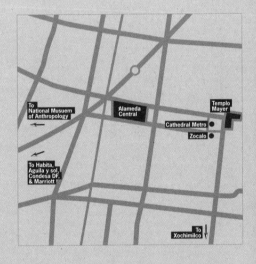

✦ Regional Information

Mexico City, the capital of Mexico, is rich in cultural heritage. Its vibrancy and colour are evident wherever you look. It has a certain spirit that soaks itself into the art, the architecture, the food and the literature. Mexico is covered with murals, littered with galleries and carries a deep folk art tradition. Its ancient civilisations have created some of the most spectacular architecture ever built, and important archaeological sites, such as the Templo Mayor and Teotihuacán, can still be visited today. There are many other archaeological sites to explore for cultural travellers, and for those who enjoy the buzz of one of the world's busiest cities, numerous excellent restaurants and bars.

There are several museums of interest in and around Mexico City. One such museum in particular is the Musuem of Frida Kahlo - one of the world's most renowned and controversial painters. Frida Kahlo (July 6th, 1907 - July 13th, 1954) was married to Diego Rivera, another influential and controversial painter. They once lived in the salubrious and charming area of San Angel in Mexico City. Diego's studio, where the artists used to paint, was used to film blockbuster movie Frida starring Salma Hayek. This studio was designed by an architect friend and painter, Juan O'Gorman, and was built with two separate dwellings (the other being Frida Kahlo's residence) interconnected by a roof terrace, making the house quite unusual for that era.

A visit to Frida's Museum is not to be missed. The museum is also part of her former house. You can see a wide range of her personal art, as well as areas of her house she spent days crippled by disease. It's quite shocking and disturbing in parts, but those who already know the artist will find it fascinating.

The Dolores Olmedo Patino outdoor museum, which exhibits some work from Frida Kahlo, as well as her socialite friends, is not to be missed. It is set in a wonderful 17th century hacienda with extensive gardens. This outdoor museum also has some interesting animals roaming around, such as the grey hairless dogs. But try not to get too close, as they can be fierce. The local youth hostel (see Stylish Essentials) next to the cathedral can arrange tours to visit the museum.

These tours can include a day trip to Xochimilco Ecological Park, often referred to as the 'Venice of Mexico' due to its beautiful and colourful canals. The park is approximately 23 km south of Mexico City. Travellers can tour the canals by boat and you can arrange to have an authentic lunch on board (usually chicken, rice and *molle*, a kind of chocolate sauce). Locals tend to hire boats for celebrations like birthday parties and local *mariachi* bands are always playing nearby, all of which adds to the entertainment.

Much closer to the city centre is the National Museum of Anthropology, which is opposite Chapultepec Park and houses the largest collection of ancient Mexican pieces in the world. There are 23 permanent exhibit halls, that have replicas of archaeological scenes: murals in the Teotihuacan exhibit and tombs in the Oaxaca and Maya rooms. This gives you the chance to see the pieces in the context in which they were found. Archaeology exhibits are located on the ground floor and ethnographical exhibits (about present day indigenous groups in Mexico) are on the upper level. The museum also has incredible Aztec rooms and ample collections from the other great civilisations that flourished much earlier in MesoAmerica.

Top left. Frida Kahlo Museum.
Top right. Cathedral Metropolitana.

Adventure: Culture Vulture
Destination: Mexico City

If you are in the Chapultepec Park area, you might also find a visit to the Zoo an interesting experience. There is an open-air bus that takes you into the park from the main square and stops off en-route to various locations (see Stylish Essentials).

Approximately 30 miles north east of Mexico City are the ancient city ruins of Teotihuacán. Like many of the archaeological sites in Mexico, Teotihuacán guards secrets we have yet to unravel. One of the greatest mysteries surrounding Teotihuacán is that no one really knows what happened to the huge population that once lived there.

Archaeological scholars, however, agree that it is probably Mexico's most important archeological site. Although the origins of Teotihuacán are uncertain, it is thought some of the inhabitants arrived from the Valley of Mexico to the south, refugees from an eruption of the Xitle volcano that caused major devastation and forced the survivors in that region to seek a new place to settle. Construction of the city probably started in the first two centuries BC, and the civilization reached its high point between 350 and 650 AD. This site was also a place where human sacrifices were made, often in correlation to astronomical events. When the site was excavated, many tombs were found, some with the remains of what were believed to be people sacrificed to the gods. There are many examples of these sacrifices across some of the other archaeological sites of Mexico.

Today, many people believe that Teotihuacán is a place of energy, and it is quite common to witness people meditating at the top of main pyramids (the Pyramid of the Sun and the Pyramid of the Moon). A visit to Teotihuacán is essential if you plan to visit Mexico on an archaeological tour; from an historical perspective, it is one of the most important archaeological sites in the world.

Museo del Templo Mayor, located in the central part of Mexico City, sits on the most sacred site of the entire Aztec Empire. The museum holds 7,000 pieces (not all displayed) unearthed from some ruins throughout central Mexico including sculptures, reliefs, skulls and other items from the Templo Mayor itself. The museum has eight halls. The halls in the South Wing are dedicated to Huitzilopochtli, the God of War, and the halls in the North Wing to Tláloc, the God of Rain. It is a fascinating museum that gives a great overview on Aztec civilisation, so well worth a visit if you are in the city centre.

Shopping in Mexico City is like any other major city, with leading designer brands from Louis Vuitton to Dior and Gucci. If shopping is your fixation, the city has numerous bazaars, plazas, malls and exclusive boutiques where you'll find crafts, brand name clothes and jewellery. In the neighbourhoods of Coyoacan and San Angel, you can enjoy a bohemian atmosphere, while in Santa Fe and Polanco you'll experience the glamour of trendy boutiques and modern hotels.

⤳ Stylish Places to Stay

Hip Style: Habita. Situated in the business district not far from the Zoo, Habita is cool, hip and trendy. This little oasis has one of the city's only rooftop swimming pools, which makes it a perfect escape from the smog and dirt of the city below. Once you have had a long day exploring the city's sights, it's a relief to dip your toes in cool water. At night this rooftop turns into a funky bar area for the trendy young crowd. Habita also has a little gym and great breakfast. But be warned this place is not for those who like peace and quiet or an early night. ⍟

Chic Style: Condesa DF, The sister hotel to Habita. Well known for its 'in' crowd and late night rooftop parties, it has an excellent restaurant serving typical Mexican food in a courtyard style setting and also a sushi bar. The architecture is very chic and the interiors minimalist.

Shoppers Style: JW Marriott. Friendly staff and a luxury setting await you at this hotel. Set in the Polanco district, it is perfect for shoppers and for those who wish to wine and dine. The hotel is part of a chain, but don't let that put you off - it has been cited by many travellers as one of the best Marriott hotels in the world.

🍽 Delicious Places to Eat

Contemporary Mexican: Aguila y sol. Marta Ortiz Chapa owns and heads up this stylish and contemporary restaurant. She is the author of eight cookbooks on regional Mexican cuisine, so she certainly has the experience. Here's your chance to try indigenous produce with a new spin, such as an appetizer of tortitas de huauzontle with goats' cheese, parmesan, and a chile pasilla sauce, or a main course of salmon in a maize crust with clams. Watch out for the spicy chilli-margarita, it will blow you head off! ⍟

Traditional Mexican: Cafe de Tacuba. This 90-year-old venue is decorated with traditional hand-painted tiles and has loads of atmosphere with live music to energise your evening. Try the delectable enchiladas verdes (casseroled maize tortillas) and green chilaquiles (very similar to enchiladas). Both dishes are made with tortilla, chicken, cream and cheese, and are covered with green sauce. Great washed down with Mexican beer.

Music & Mexican: Hostería Santo Domingo. Chamber music fills the room at this hugely popular restaurant. Based in a former monastery in the Centro Historico, it has a beautiful stained glass windows on the ground floor designed by the painter Jose Gomez Rosas. The visitors' book contains the signatures of many well-known local politicians, artists, intellectuals, businessmen and sportsmen. Try the quesadillas they are delicious.

Adventure: Nature Lover
Destination: Yucatán Peninsula

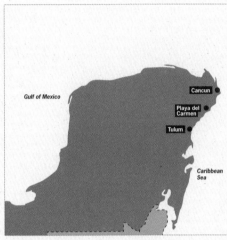

Gulf of Mexico

Cancun

Playa del Carmen

Tulum

Caribbean Sea

Regional Information

Temples, hills and beaches are plentiful in Mexico, and nowhere is this truer than on the Yucatan peninsular. The area includes some excellent attractions, such as the thriving tourist destination of Cancún, the wild flamingos in Celestun, the ancient Mayan archaeological sites of Chichen Itza and Tulum, the beautiful town of Playa del Carmen, the quaint fishing village of Puerto Morelos, and the state capital Merida.

You can get to the area overland from the south via Belize and Guatemala, although most visitors find it more convenient to fly to Cancún airport directly from Mexico City, or to another regional airport such as Veracruz, Tux Tla Guitierrez, or nearby Merida. If you want the freedom to explore the area, then hiring a car is your best option. We would recommend a stay of at least ten days to see the region's highlights.

Until the 1960s, the Yucatán Peninsula was largely a cattle ranching and horticultural production area. Since the 1970s, the Yucatán has reoriented its economy towards tourism, especially in Quintana Roo. Once a small fishing village, Cancún in the north east of the peninsula has grown into a thriving tourist destination. The Riviera Maya, which stretches along the east coast of the peninsula between Cancún and Tulum, currently has more than 50,000 beds and is visited by many thousands of tourists every year. Cancún's man-made beaches and chain hotels attract mostly package holidaymakers. There are, however, a variety of wonderful and unusual places to stay in the Peninsular for those wanting a more local and off-the-beaten-track experience.

The Yucatán Peninsular offers beautiful natural environments, such as Celestun, the natural habitat for hundreds of pink flamingos, or Ria Lagartos, where you can go kayaking through the mangroves. You can visit both nesting areas in a day but visit during October and November for the best chance of seeing the flamingos.

Mexico's flamingo population is on the rise having been rescued from the threat of extinction by a Yucatán based environmental group. Yucatán is home to Mesoamerica's only flamingo population living in the wild. Although flamingos can fly great distances, sometimes migrating as far as Florida's Everglades, they rarely leave Yucatán's warm, shallow inland waters. Yucatan's flamingos were endangered before the Mexican government declared two areas - Ria Lagartos and Ria Celestun - off limits in 1979. The government spent $45,000 to rebuild one of the peninsula's most important flamingo nesting sites in order to protect it from flooding. An island in Ria Lagartos Biosphere Reserve, called Punta Mecoh, or Flamingo Point, is now covered with a fresh layer of shell fragments and clay like sand that flamingos use to build their nests. Last year, 10,000 flamingo chicks were hatched in the reserve.

There are many Mayan archaeological sites throughout the peninsula. Some of the better known ones are Chichen Itza (a UNESCO world heritage site), Tikal, Tulum and Uxmal. Indigenous Maya and Mestizos of partial Mayan descent still make up a sizeable portion of the region's population, and Mayan languages are still widely spoken there.

The ancient and mystical Mayan capital Chichen Itza attracts thousands of tourists every year. It is located 75 miles from Merida, and is best visited first thing in the morning - before the crowds arrive and before the sun gets too hot. You can stay overnight virtually outside the entrance if you want to avoid the queues. The name Chichen Itza is a Mayan word meaning 'mouth' (Chi), 'well' (Chen) and 'Itza' (of the Itza tribe). Some authorities believe people were thrown into the nearby 'cenotes' (water holes) as sacrifices, and those who survived were treated as seers (people who see the future).

Adventure: Nature Lover
Destination: Yucatán Peninsula

The main pyramid at Chichen Itza is El Castillo. Visitors used to be able to climb the steep steps, but this was abolished in January 2006. However, it is sometimes still possible to visit the inside passageway of the pyramid. Just beyond El Castillo there is a large ball court where Mayan men played a game called 'Pok ta Pok'. It is believed that the object of the game was to throw a ball in the air through a ring that was mounted on the wall 7m above the ground. At the entrance to Chichen Itza there is a museum, dining room and gift shops. Tulum, 1.5 hours south of Cancun, has an impressive setting on the beach with the Caribbean waves crashing along the coast. Its archaeological sites might not be as large and inspiring as Chichen Itza, but the location is superb. This is the only Mayan site to be in use at the time of the Spanish conquest in the 16th century. Tulum actually means 'wall' in Mayan and is believed to have acted as a defence system, which is perhaps the reason why it sits on a 15 metre high cliff above the sea. There is a lovely beach to stop by for a picnic and a swim. In fact, the Tulum area has fantastic white beaches that are less touristy then other parts of coastline. The town of Tulum is attractive and up-and-coming, so it's worth staying a night there if you intend to visit the site.

Playa del Carmen is another popular tourist spot, but you would never guess it. Although it is one of Mexico's fastest growing cities, it still has a laid-back fishing village atmosphere. There are some fantastic restaurants, bars, hip hotels and great boutique shops selling local arts, crafts and hammocks. Visitors are attracted to this town (and quite rightly so) because it has gorgeous stretches of white sand, a relaxed pace of life while still being relatively busy.

Puerto Morelos is a small fishing village. The pier in the centre of the village hosts snorkel and sport fishing boats, while yachts dock in a man-made harbour just to the south. Puerto Morelos used to be the embarkation point for the car ferry to Cozumel, a nearby island, but the ferry now leaves from Calica, a major port south of Playa del Carmen. Mexico recently declared the coral reefs that fringe the coast near Puerto Morelos as a national marine park as part of the Great Maya Reef. Snorkelers and divers have long frequented the area and while the rest of the coast is suffering from over-development, Puerto Morelos remains one of the most tranquil small villages in the country.

During your stay in the Peninsular, you should also visit the state capital, Merida, where you can stroll down the main avenue, Paseo Montejo, which is lined with beautiful palaces, old buildings and 19th century mansions. All this makes the so-called 'White City' one of the most visited destinations in the country. In the surrounding areas, you can stay in old haciendas, many of which have been converted into luxurious hotels with museums, restaurants and spa services.

⤴ Stylish Places to Stay

Local Style: Hacienda Chichen. This gorgeously converted hacienda near Chichen Itza is family run and dates back to the 16th century. The archaeologists who excavated Chichen Itza lived here during the 1920s. Since then, it has been renovated without losing any of its character.

Hip Style: Mezanine. Situated on Tulum's gorgeous beach facing stretches of white sand, this is a wonderful getaway destination. It's modern, intimate and hip, making it a refreshing change from old-style hacienda accommodation. The suites are very spacious and feature natural stone rain showers and fluffy bath towels. ★

Deluxe Style: Paraiso de la Bonita. Head south from Cancún towards Playa de Carmen to find beautiful hidden beaches and sleepy towns. Here there is a beautiful sanctuary, Paraiso de la Bonita, near Puerto Morelos. Although a 'high society' crowd frequents it, it is wonderfully relaxing, discreet and unpretentious. Each room is themed and has private plunge pools, decadent marble bathrooms, complete with designer toiletries. ★ .

🍴 Delicious Places to Eat

Cool & Hip: Deseo Lounge. This is a fun and hip place for pre-dinner drinks, light food and snacks while watching the world go by in Playa del Carmen. It has a great rooftop swimming pool and bar.

Best Italian: Posada Margherita. Strange as it may seem to see an Italian restaurant as one of our best picks, the food and service here rival anywhere in Rome. This eco-friendly hotel in Tulum has the best Italian restaurant in Mexico, without a doubt. Try the selection of homemade breads dipped in balsamic and oil, with great cheese and wine.

Best authentic Yucatecan: Yaxche. One of the most authentic restaurants in the peninsular, this eatery in Playa del Carmen is considered something of an institution.

Adventure: Rest + Relaxation
Destination: Los Cabos
(Southern Baja California)

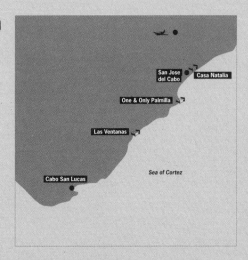

Regional Information

Los Cabos, or 'Cabo' as the Americans call it, is a superb getaway for those looking for a romantic escape, butler service, year-round sunny climate and white sandy beaches. The corridor along the coast is made up of two very distinctive towns, Cabo San Lucas and San Jose del Cabo, which are very different from one another. San Jose del Cabo is quiet and laid-back and features shady relaxed courtyard restaurants and Spanish-style buildings. Cabo San Lucas, on the other hand, is a wild party town with shopping plazas and nightclubs. Between the towns lies an incredible coastline with gorgeous beaches, exclusive hotels and spas to pamper your every whim.

Situated at the very tip of Baja California, Los Cabos is only a short flight from Mexico City or Los Angeles. The Hollywood jet-set crowd and discerning travellers are mainly attracted to this area due to its party scene, elite hotels, golf courses and spas. Baja California is famous for its constant warm temperatures. It is also a good choice for those wanting to get away from it all by relaxing on a hammock or sunbathing under the hot sun.

Getting to Los Cabos is easy and stress-free. You can catch a short flight from Mexico City, or you can fly directly from Los Angeles. It's not uncommon for some holiday makers to hire a private jet - many land here on a daily basis.

It is also easy to get to your hotel. If you plan ahead and don't want the hassle of transport when you get there, you can ask one of the many taxis to take you up to your front door. Some of the elite hotels have their own fleet service, which guarantees that you arrive in style. A week should be enough to make sure you are fully relaxed. However, if you are going to explore more of the region and have flown long-haul beforehand then two weeks is ideal.

Adventure: Rest + Relaxation
Destination: Los Cabos
(Southern Baja California)

The highlights of the area are its natural beaches, clear blue sea and year-round sunny climate. There are also plenty of activities for water sports enthusiasts including diving, surfing and fishing. If shopping is your thing, there are plenty of market stalls selling locally made products such as hammocks, pottery, art and Mexican leather boots. When the sun goes down, eating out and drinking are the most popular past-times. This is the kind of place where you can sit on the beach, still in your swimsuit, watch the sun set and drink cocktails.

El Arco (the arch), a jagged feature that partially fills the tide, is where the Sea of Cortez meets the Pacific Ocean creating a wonderful colour in the sea. This is one of the region's finest sites and inevitably attracts a lot of tourists. Pelican sea lions can usually be seen here, playing in the sea. If you are scuba diving, you usually pass El Arco on your way to the numerous dive sites in the area.

The colonial style Iglesia San José, built in the 1730s, is a highlight of the town of San José del Cabo. It is situated on the central square near the local market. It's worth a look if you are visiting the town, particularly early in the evening when the sun dips behind the trees. It is also a great spot for people watching, and there is nothing better than downing a tequila in a nearby café.

The stretches of beaches that run along the Cabo Corridor are incredibly picturesque, especially with the Sea of Cortez as your backdrop. The longest beach is 3 km, which is great for strolling or running. The most romantic spot is Playa el Bledito, where most of the elite resorts are based. Despite there being a catalogue of deluxe hotels here, you still feel very secluded.

Opposite page. Top. Poolside at Las Ventanas. **Bottom.** Mi Casa restaurant.

⤴ Stylish Places to Stay

Poolside Chic: Las Ventanas. Clean and minimalist, this hotel is a haven for those who want to relax in fuss-free surroundings. All the suites are decorated using simple colours and materials. The incredible infinity pool and flawless service give this place the chic and style of Los Cabos without the pretence. ☆

Grand Charm: One & Only Palmilla. An enormous resort-style setting with everything you can imagine, from a 27-hole golf course to a hotel chapel. It's so grand that you need a golf buggy to get around. What this place lacks in intimacy it makes up for in pure luxury and indulgence. The hammocks on the beach and the cabanas with a private butler ensure you don't need to lift a finger.

Local Style: Casa Natalia. Small, intimate and romantic. Only 16 rooms, decorated with indigenous arts and crafts. If you are looking for something more secluded and friendly, this place has real personality.

🍽 Delicious Places to Eat

Local delights: Mi Casa. Hidden down a small side street in Cabo San Lucas, this huge Hacienda structure with a stunning courtyard is brightly decorated with local crafts - which are also sold in the art shop. The freshly prepared seafood is delicious and *mariachis* entertain you while you eat. ☆

Courtyard Chic: Tequila Restaurant. This restaurant offers a romantic and magical setting for an intimate dinner. The dining area is a large candlelit rear patio with mature fruit trees and a fragrant herb garden. Located in charming San José del Cabo, the service is impeccable, as is the Beef Tenderloin in Cabernet.

Mexican fun: Panchos Restaurant. Pancho's is colourful and brightly decorated with hand painted murals and memorabilia. Located in Cabo San Lucas, it claims to have the world's largest collection of Tequilas - over 575 expertise types.

Focus On...
Yoga retreat at Bay of Banderas (Verana)

Located 30 miles south of Puerto Vallarta, floating above the Bay of Banderas, carved out of lush Mexican jungle on a hillside is Verana - a luxury yoga retreat. It is as unusual as it is remote and has a unique design that is rustic yet sophisticated. Verana has been designed for travellers with a sense of adventure and an appreciation of tranquility and natural beauty.

To access the retreat is a mission in itself, you actually need to walk miles through the Mexican jungle (although the mule will be on hand to carry your luggage). Verana is a wonderful retreat with daily yoga sessions, private plunge pools and the service is so good that when you return to your room after dinner the staff light up your house with hundreds of tea-light candles.

The rooms may be a little primitive (there are no safes, mini-bar, hairdryer or door key) but you won't be spending much time in them as there are plenty of things to do - such as daily hikes to the beach, massages in the spa, and swimming. A word of warning though, don't come here expecting to lose weight, the food is that good you may end up piling on the pounds. This place is quite an adventure in itself and makes an excellent start to any travel trip.

Should pack:
• Good water hiking shoes like Tevas or Keens. Your feet get wet getting in and out of the water taxi.
• Bathing suits and cover-up.
• Shorts & T-shirts. Only if you will be doing some hiking, going on excursions or walking to Yelapa - which is at least a 30 minute walk from Verana back down the hill.
• Bug spray and sunscreen.
• Hair dryer.
• Torches.

Don't pack:
• Shoes that are not easy to walk in.
• Too much makeup. It's too dark at night to see anything at night, anyway.
• Big bulky backpacks. Something to hold a water bottle is fine for the short hikes. A smaller backpack to hold the water and a light lunch would work if you are looking at more serious hikes.
• Dressy clothes.

(i) Stylish Essentials

General Information
www.visitmexico.com

UK Embassy
Río Lerma 71
www.embajadabritanica.com.mx
T. +55 5242 8500 (info)

Airlines

Aero Mexico Airline
www.aeromexico.com
T. 0207 801 6234 (UK Info)

Mexicana Airlines
www.mexicana.com
T. +1 800 531 7921

(USA Reservation Line)

Aero Calafia
www.aereocalafia.com.mx

Aero California
www.aerocalifornia.com
T. +1 800 237 6225 (from Mexico)

Alaska Airlines
www.alaskaair.com
T. +1 800 252 7522 (from USA)

American Airlines
www.aa.com
T. 0207 365 0777 (UK Reservations)

British Airways
www.ba.com
T. 0870 850 9850 (UK Reservations)

Continental
www.continental.com
T. 0845 607 6760 (UK Help line)

Delta Airlines
www.delta.com
T. 0845 600 0950 (UK reservations)

Great Rail Journeys
www.greatrailuk.com
T. 0845 402 2068 (For information
and booking)

Avis Car Hire
www.avis.com

**Private Transfers to get you over
the borders**
www.gettransfers.com
T. +52 501 422 2485
E. gettransfers@gmail.com

Mexico City

YHA Tours
www.mexicocityhostel.com

**Open-air top bus tour
Turibus Mexico**
http://64.78.37.75/turibus/
contactanos.html

Ecological Park of Xochimilco
www.xochimilco.df.gob.mx
(Spanish Only)
T. +52 55 56738061
Open: 9.00 am – 6.00 pm

National Museum of Anthropology
Paseo de la Reforma, opposite
Chapultepec Park main entrance
www.mna.inah.gob.mx
Open: Tue-Sun 9.00 am – 7.00 pm
Cost: admission 38 pesos
nearest metro: Chapultepec

Teotihuacán
http://archaeology.asu.edu/teo/
T. +52 55 956 02 76
Open: 9.00 am – 4.00 pm

Xochimilco
www.xochimilco.df.gob.mx
(Spanish Only)

Museo del Templo Mayor
www.conaculta.gob.mx/templomayor
(Spanish Only)
E. difusion.mntm@inah.gob.mx
Open: Mon-Fri 11.00 am – 4.00 pm

Habita Hotel
www.hotelhabita.com
T. +52 55 5282 3100

Condesa D.F Hotel
www.condesadf.com
T. +52 55 5241 2600

Marriott Hotel
www.marriott.com/hotels/travel/
mexjw-jw-marriott-hotel-mexico-city/
T. +52 55 5999 0000

Aguila y Sol
Águila y Sol 42 Avenida Molière,
Polanco Mexico City
T. +52 55 5281 8354
Open: Dinner

Hostería Santo Domingo
Domínguez 72
www.hosteriadesantodomingo.com.mx
T. +52 55 265276 (info)
Open: Mon - Sat 9.00 am – 10.00 pm

Cafe Tacuba
Tacuba 28 about 3 blocks from
Palacio de Bellas Artes, west on
Tacuba just past Bolivar
T. +52 5518 4950
Open: Daily 8.00 am – 11.30 pm

Yucatan Peninsular

General Information
www.visitmexico.com/wb/
Visitmexico/Visi_Yucatan
www.travelyucatan.com

**Eco Tours in the Yucatan
Peninsular**
www.ecoyuc.com/kayaking.html
T. +52 999 9202772

Chichen Itza
Entrance near Hacienda Chichen
Open: 7 Days a week
8.00 am – 5.00 pm

Tulum Ruins
Parque Nationale Tulum
Open: Daily 7.00 am – 5.00 pm

Hacienda Chichen Itza
www.haciendachichen.com
T. +52 999 920 8407

Mezanine
www.mezzanine.com.mx
T. +52 998 1122 845

Paraiso de la Bonita
www.paraisodelabonita.com
T. +52 998 872 8300

Deseo Hotel + Lounge
5a Av. Y Calle 12, Playa del Carmen
www.hoteldeseo.com
T. +52 984 879 3620
Open: Evening dinner

Posada Margherita
Carretera Tulum-Boca Paila Km. 4,5
www.posadamargherita.com
T. +52 984 801 8493
Open: Daily until midnight.
Closed Sundays

Yaxche
Calle 8, playa del Carmen
T. +52 984 873 2502
Open: Daily 12:00 pm - 12:00 am

Los Cabos - Baja California

General Information
www.loscabosguide.com

Diving Schools
www.cabodiving.com/divesites.html

Surfing Schools
www.cabosurfhotel.com

Las Ventanas
www.lasventanas.com
T. +52 624 144 2800

One & Only Palmilla
www.oneandonlypalmilla.com
T. +52 624 146 7000

Casa Natalia
www.slh.com
T. +52 624 146 7100

Tequila Restaurant
Manuel Doblado #1011 between
Boulevard Mijares and Hidalgo
T. +52 624 142 1155
F. +52 624 142 3753
Open: Daily 6.00 pm – 11.00 pm

Mi Casa Restaurant
Located just off Lázaro Cárdenas,
Cabo San Lucas
T. +52 624 143 1933 (Reservations)
E. salesmicasa@gmail.com
Open: Daily Noon – 3.00 pm
(except Sunday) 5.30 pm – 10.30 pm

Panchos Restaurant
Hidalgo Street, one block from Marina
Boulevard, Cabo San Lucas
T. +52 624 143 0973
F. +52 624 143 509
Open: Daily 8.00 am – 11.00 pm

Verana
Calle Zaragoza #404, Colonia Centro
Puerto Vallarta, Jalisco 48304, MX
www.verana.com
T. +52 310.360.0155
F. +52 310.360.0158

Whale watching in Kaikoura

NEW ZEALAND

Northeast | Southwest & Queenstown |
Christchurch, Canterbury & Marlborough |
Abel Tasman

🏆 Why is this place so special?

New Zealand is a country of great beauty, glaciers, mountain ranges, giant waterfalls, deep blue lakes, hissing geysers and boiling mud. It also contains dense forests, deserted beaches and a variety of fauna, such as the kiwi that are endemic to its shores. As soon as you land in the country, you sense its serenity, its vast outdoor spaces and closeness to nature.

It is no wonder that New Zealand offers all of this natural beauty - the country is about the same size of the UK but has a population of just 3.8 million people - three quarters of whom live in the North Island.

There are, on average, 13 people per square km (compared to a staggering 243 people per square km in the UK). As such, New Zealand has plenty of isolated places to explore, without seeing another human being for miles.

The two main islands, the North Island and the South Island, offer adventures for a variety of travellers, including action-thrill seekers, walkers, climbers and foodies. Both the islands are vastly different from one another.

The North Island is much smaller in area than the South Island but it has a larger population, centred on the capital Wellington, and the major city Auckland. The North Island is the centre of New Zealand's arts and culture scene. There is the Maori Arts and Crafts institute in Rotorua as well national art galleries in Auckland and Wellington, which offer some strong contemporary art. The North Island also has some stunning under-rated scenery and beaches, such as Hot Water Beach in Coromandel, where you can dig deep into the sand in order to create your own hot water pool. Finally, the North Island is home to the magnificent cave systems in Waitomo near Wiakato.

The South Island has breathtaking scenery, huge mountain ranges (including the Southern Alps), national parks, quaint towns (such as Arrowtown) and notable glaciers, such as Tasman Glacier and Hooker glacier located on Mount Cook. Another notable feature of the South Island is its myriad rivers and lakes: notably the Whanganui River and the breathtaking lakes, Waikaremoana, Taupo and Wanaka, which make it an excellent destination for those who enjoy outdoor adventures. Canterbury - the gateway to the South Island - is where you can experience the wonder of whale watching in Kaikoura, or head towards Marlborough for exquisite food and wine. The Southwest coast allows you to walk on glaciers, through natural bush, or simply wander some of the most beautiful, rugged tracks on earth.

Any number of vigorous outdoor activities including glacier hiking, skiing, rafting and, of course, that perennial favourite, bungy jumping for the brave. Those who aren't such dare devils can swim with dolphins, whale-watch, drink fine wine and eat wonderfully fresh food.

New Zealand has long been a favourite for clued-up travellers thanks to its spectacular scenery, welcoming people and ease of travelling around. Recently it has been given a 'must-go' status in many travel publications. This position has been cemented by the success of The Lord Of The Rings, which was filmed entirely in New Zealand. To explore the wonders and activities that New Zealand has to offer, we would recommend a trip of at least three weeks.

📋 Fast Facts

Capital: Wellington.

Location: Situated to the south-east of Australia in the Pacific Ocean.

Population: 4,000,000

Religion: 75% Christianity, 25% other.

Language: English.

Getting there and exploring around

Getting to New Zealand from the UK is easy. You can usually buy an air ticket to the country as part of a round-the-world ticket, making it economical to stop off at other destinations en-route, for example Australia, the Pacific Islands or somewhere in Asia. The best way to get around New Zealand is by road or by train. Hiring a campervan or car and staying at lodges will allow you get the maximum coverage. It will also give you the flexibility to pack up and move on whenever and wherever you please. You can choose from 4 - 12 birth campervans, with all the luxury amenities from microwaves to showers. Roads are well built in the main towns, although beware of hairpin bends and icy conditions in the winter. If you wish to visit both the North and South Islands, you can take your car or camper across the notoriously choppy 'Cook Strait' by ferry, but book in advance (especially during summer season) to guarantee a place.

Travelling by luxury coach is another relaxing way of seeing the countryside. You have the option of a group tour or individual tour tickets which have been especially designed for the independent traveller.

New Zealand also has several train journeys that are an excellent way to see its scenic highlights. Horizon Holidays has several tour packages that incorporate these train journeys.

Best time of year to visit

Although New Zealand can be visited at any time of year because of its beautiful warm summers and cool clear winters, the North and the South island experience distinctively different patterns of rainfall because of their different geological features. On the South Island, the Southern Alps act as a barrier for moisture-laden winds coming from the Tasman Sea, which create a wet climate to the west of the mountains and a dry climate to the east. At the same time, the North Island's rainfall is more evenly distributed and more consistent. Temperatures are a few degrees cooler in the South Island, and both islands receive snow in the winter.

Winter falls in the months of June to August, and summer from December to February. It is important to remember that New Zealand's climate is maritime, rather than continental, which means the weather can change with amazing rapidity. So be on your guard while driving.

The busy tourist season falls in the warmer months between November and April, though ski resorts, such as Queenstown, are busy during winter. If you're travelling during peak periods (especially the Christmas season) it's best to book ahead, as much accommodation and transport fill up. It's probably more pleasant to visit either before or after this hectic period, when the weather is still warm and there aren't as many other travellers around.

? Must know before you go

Plan ahead. If you are planning a trip to New Zealand, it is advisable to plan in advance to make the most of the country. During the high season (summer), popular places such as Rotorua and Queenstown can become very crowded. So plan activities and accommodation before your trip.

Declare everything. Bio security is a buzzword for New Zealand's customs officers - the authorities are serious about keeping out any diseases that may harm the country's agricultural industry. Hiking gear such as boots and tents will be checked and may need to be cleaned before being allowed in. You must declare any plant or animal products (including anything made of wood), and food of any kind. You'll also come in for extra scrutiny if you've arrived via Africa, South East Asia or South America.

Bring clothing to suit any conditions. Because the North and South Island climates can change without notice, it is wise to always bring a few layers of thermal clothing. You can always send a parcel home if you are travelling to a warmer climate later. Temperatures can range from subtropical in the North to temperate in the South: summer daytime temperatures are between 60-85°F, (15-29°C), while winter temperatures range from 40-60°F, (4-15°C).

🐚 Highlights

Festivals and Events. Wine Marlborough Festival (Second weekend in February; Blenheim); Golden Shears Sheep-Shearing Contest (March; Masterton), a must for lovers of sheep and sweat; and Canterbury Show Week (November; Christchurch), which has agricultural exhibits, rides and local entertainment.

Ice climbing. Head to the Franz Josef glacier on the west coast region of the South Island, for some incredibly scenic hikes on crisp, fresh glaciers. Be assured this is jaw-dropping scenery, and the exciting helicopter ride to the top will be a major highlight.

Bungy Jumping. This past time is the nation's most celebrated adrenaline rush. There is nothing quite like throwing yourself off the transparent platform of the 'Nevis Bungy', near Queenstown, once you've done the jump, you won't be able to take the smile off your face for a week!

Wine tour. New Zealand has some of the best wine in the world. Don't miss visiting a few wineries in the Marlborough region or Hawke's Bay.

From top. Sheep in the road, Inside the Maori House, geysers in Rotorua.

Adventure: Nature Lover
Destination: Northeast
(Coromandel, Waikato, Rotorua & Lake Taupo)

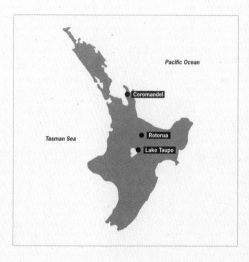

Pacific Ocean

Coromandel

Tasman Sea

Rotorua

Lake Taupo

✦ Regional Information

The North Island of New Zealand is perhaps best known for the unique volcanic plateau at its centre. This thermal belt contains active volcanoes - Ruapehu, Ngauruhoe and Tongariro - and magnificent examples of geysers, boiling mud pools, hot springs and steam vents. In Waitomo District, the Waitomo Caves - with their caverns, underground rivers and glittering glow-worms - are one of the island's most popular attractions. In the Northeast, the fabulous Coromandel is famous for its scenic islands, beaches and secluded coves. The North Island is packed with national parks, thermal fields, hot springs, ski areas, native forests, rivers and historic Maori sites, making it an excellent destination for those who enjoy unusual scenery, natural wonders and a little culture.

Coromandel is rustic, relaxed and unspoiled; the Coromandel is one of New Zealand's best-loved holiday destinations. It is quite a drive from Auckland, so you may wish to spend a night somewhere en-route, but once there you could settle for a couple of days and soak up the rugged volcanic hills and more than 400 km of spectacular coastline. Coromandel is a place where bush and beach are easily accessible. In the same day you can experience the blue dazzle of the Pacific Ocean and the calming greenness of the Kauri forest.

Inspired by Coromandel's idyllic setting, many artists and crafts people have made the region their home. Visitors to the area are welcome in the studios of these artists. The area's fascinating history is evident in gold mining relics, logging dams and ancient Maori sites. The region's past can also be explored in the charming colonial architecture and historical buildings preserved in several towns around the region.

One of the most renowned attractions in the Northeast is Hot Water beach, where visitors can hire a spade and head out towards the sea at low tide to dig out their own bathing pool. The natural minerals are reportedly good for your skin. Volcanic activity is no longer prevalent on the Coromandel Peninsula - the hot mineral pools are a legacy of an exciting geothermal past. Hot Water Beach is also known as a good surfing spot.

Cathedral Cove is another hotspot for visitors. The walk along the dramatic coastline is superb. The Cathedral Cove is extremely secluded - it is only accessible by foot or by boat - and as such you may well find that you are the only person on the beach. It is easy to reach and clearly signposted from Coromandel town.

The region of Waikato is an area of rolling hills - which are used for dairy and sheep farming and racehorse breeding - large areas of native bush and distant mountains. In addition to being a small friendly place, it offers an enormous range of attractions, adventures and everlasting memories of a silent world. This area is truly a natural scenic wonder.

Waitomo, with its vast network of caves, is testament to a time when parts of New Zealand lay under the sea. These cave systems - sinkholes and underground streams - provide huge scope for exploration and adventure. They are one of New Zealand's most commanding wonders and are a celebration of mother nature's work - glow-worms, stalactites and stalagmites which have developed over the last 100,000 years. A guided tour will take you through stunning underground scenery, including the Cathedral with its perfect acoustics. The best tour company to use is The Black Water Rafting Company. However, don't even think about going caving unless you are comfortable with restricted heights and climbing. Some tours involve abseiling 90 metres into a lost world and jumping on black water tubes in complete darkness while floating through underground streams. After you have spent a day in the freezing caves, you may want to head towards Rotorua for some hot mud therapy. Waitomo is situated less than 80 km to the south of Hamilton in the Waikato region, so can be visited during the day from Rotorua or Lake Taupo.

Many travellers tend to flock towards Rotorua, because it is considered to be the Maori's spiritual home. It offers visitors a chance to free their spirit at one of the many spectacular lakes, rejuvenate at one of the many natural geothermal complexes around the city, challenge their spirit with a burst of adrenalin, experience the living Maori culture both in the contemporary and traditional sense, and feel the earth as it rumbles beneath their feet. It you don't make it to Rotura, you can experience Maori culture in other parts of the country, such as Waitangi, the Museum of New Zealand Te Papa Tongarewa in Wellington, and the National Marae in Christchurch.

Maori people often use the term 'tangata whenua', or 'people of the land' to describe themselves. This term emphasises their relationship with a particular area of land. The Maori have a close kinship with their environment and legends and gods represent certain worlds, such as Tane Mahuta (God of the Forest) and Tangaroa (God of the Sea). These gods are remembered through song and dance. The marae, or meeting house, is still today the main focus for ceremony and communal identity for Maori people. Visitors are welcomed onto the marae with a strict formal protocol and traditional welcome, which includes the haka (challenge) and a hongi (pressing of noses). You may have the opportunity to sample kai (food), cooked in a hangi (steamed in an earth oven). This is all visible at the Rotorua Art & History Museum.

Adventure: Nature Lover
Destination: Northeast
(Coromandel, Waikato, Rotorua & Lake Taupo)

As Rotorua is a thermal area, the first thing that will hit you will be the smell of sulphur, and you won't be able to get rid of it for days. It can be said that Rotorua is one of the geothermal wonders of the world. It is full of outrageously coloured pools and lakes, and some really wild looking silicate and mineral formations. There are five main geothermal areas: Whakarewarewa, Tikitere (Hell's Gate), Waimangu, Waiotapu and Ohinemutu. Each area offers different thermal experiences, from bursting geysers to steamy lakes. At Hell's Gate you can soak in one of the private hot-mud pools, which is good for rehydrating the skin and has excellent healing properties for any skin condition. It is sizzling, smelly and serious fun.

The Waikato River is one of New Zealand's longest rivers and it drains into Lake Taupo, the largest freshwater lake in all of Australasia. The Lake Taupo region displays some of the finest examples in New Zealand of untouched, unspoilt and uncrowded country.

Tongariro National Park is the oldest national park in New Zealand and is a UNESCO world heritage site. It has active volcanic mountains - Ruapehu, Ngauruhoe and Tongariro - home to many Maori sacred sites. It is a rough and unstable environment of shrub lands, forests and rocky mountains. This is also where they filmed scenes of Lord of The Rings such as 'Mordor', and 'the Plains of Gorgoroth'. The plains themselves are vast and can be seen from either the National Park side of the park, or from the Desert Road. One of the best ways to explore this park is to walk the 17 km Tongariro crossing which has been classed in the world's top ten one-day walks by National Geographic magazine.

Huka falls are a set of waterfalls on the Waikato and are well worth visiting. A few hundred metres upstream, the Waikato River narrows in width - from roughly 100 metres to 15 metres - creating a silica canyon. The volume of water flowing through this canyon often approaches 220,000 litres per second. At the top of the falls is a set of small waterfalls dropping about 8 metres. The final stage of the falls is most impressive with an 11 metre drop. A jetboat takes tourists within a few metres of the bottom of this final stage.

⌐ Stylish Places to Stay

Luxury Style: Huka Lodge. Situated in seven hectares of park-like grounds, Huka Lodge offers 20 lodges as well as the exclusive Owner's Cottage with its four luxurious rooms - all just metres from Waikato River. Secluded and offering every comfort, from mini-bar to walk-in dressing rooms, the rooms are spacious, light and peaceful. This place has been visited by many royal figures and it's no wonder, as every bathroom has its own private garden, under floor heating and sunken baths - what more could a princess want? ★

Eco-Lux Style: Treetops Lodge. This gorgeous lodge is made from timber and stone and is located in Rotorua - it's a real sanctuary. The lodge is situated in 2,500 acres of forest and game reserve which offers over 70 km of hiking trails, mountain biking, horse riding and the ultimate in tranquillity and splendour, perfect for those who enjoy the outdoors by day and relish a stylish luxury bed for the night.

Beach Style: Colleith Lodge. This luxury five star single level boutique-style accommodation is set in a breathtaking location on the east coast of the Coromandel Peninsula. Amid native bush and built in tune with the natural environment, you get fabulous sea views, great cuisine and homely service.

⍟ Delicious Places to Eat

Prawn Charm: Prawn Farm. New Zealand's only geothermal prawn farm and home to 'Shawn the Prawn', this farm explains everything you need to know about prawns. You can also pick your own to take away or dine at the fine riverside restaurant in Huka Falls. Grab a bucket of home grown prawns and wash it down with some great New Zealand wine. ★

Seaview Seafood: Admirals Restaurant. This is the only restaurant in Coromandel with sea views. Located over the harbour, this place boasts the freshest seafood in town. It certainly lives up to its great reputation.

Gourmet Glory: Caper's Epicurean. Serving international cuisine and stocking a wide range of both local and imported goods, Caper's has everything a discerning food junkie could want. Customers can dine in the fine restaurant, or take home a gift box stuffed with condiments, biscotti and fine wine. Located in Rotorua.

Adventure: Action Hero
Destination: Southwest and Queenstown

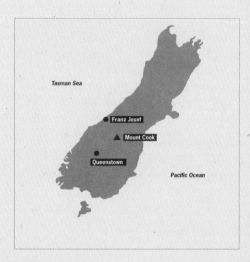

✈ Regional Information

If you like action there really is no better place to visit than New Zealand. The country is pure heaven for those who love outdoor adventures and adrenaline thrills. You can do just about anything and everything here, from bungy jumping to ice climbing, and there is no place better than the scenic Southwest Coast and Queenstown. If you have already experienced the North Island and are driving, then we recommend a minimum of a week to fully explore the area. If you are on public transport, there is also the TranzAlpine train, which arrives from Greymouth and departs daily to Christchurch. Daily transport services to and from other South Island and West Coast centres are provided by a number of coach and shuttle companies. When New Zealanders talk about the drama of landscape, they will likely mention the Southwest Coast. Sandwiched between the Tasman Sea and the Southern Alps, everything about the area is dramatic. A multitude of natural wonders await explorers, such as advancing glaciers, dense rainforests, glittering fiords, fish-filled rivers, boulder-strewn beaches and a history that includes the hunt for precious greenstone (jade), gold, coal and timber.

Greymouth is the West Coast's main commercial centre and largest town. Once the site of a major Maori Pa (fort), the town came into prominence during the great gold rush of 1865. The name Greymouth honours Sir George Grey, twice governor and once Premier of New Zealand. Visitors to Greymouth can explore 'Dragons Cave Rafting' and white-water rafting. Float in a galaxy world of glow-worms, slide across underground waterfalls, cuddle through the 'Love-Tunnel' and discover enchanting limestone formations. Also enjoy one of the 'Hot-Rock' whitewater rafting adventures for an exhilarating thrill. Greymouth is a good stopover choice for those arriving to the area.

Adventure: Action Hero
Destination: Southwest
and Queenstown

Nowhere in the world's temperate zones are glaciers as accessible as the Southwest's most famous pair of glaciers, Franz Josef and Fox. The Franz Josef Glacier is 7.5 miles long, lies to the north of its partner and is steeper. Maori legend on the creation of the glacier is beautifully encapsulated in its Maori name - Ka Koimata o Hinehukatere, 'the tears of the avalanche girl'. According to the legend, Hinehukatere loved climbing in the mountains and persuaded her lover, Tawe, to go with her. However, Tawe slipped and fell to his death. The heartbroken girl wept and her tears froze to form the glacier.

Popular trips are available onto the glacier, either by walking with a guide or by taking a helicopter flight. The best experience takes a full day when you will begin your journey with a scenic flight to the top of the glacier. The tour guide will give you a quick demonstration on how to wear your Ice Talonz (heal grips) and will guide you up, by digging out steps and tunnels in the ice. You will probably see and experience terrain normally only visited by seasoned mountaineers. This is an incredible experience, and the views of ice caves, pinnacles and the peaks of the Southern Alps are remarkable. A day in this area should be long enough or, if you want to explore longer, an overnight stay at one of the local lodges such be sufficient.

Queenstown, New Zealand's spectacular alpine resort, offers thrill-seekers a variety of experiences on many levels. Queenstown's cosmopolitan flavour is reflected in the vibrant downtown centre, where there is a myriad of restaurants and bars and the shops are open all week long. Queenstown is compact enough to walk around, with courtesy buses and taxis available to take you to outlying attractions.

There are a host of popular activities for action hero travellers staying in Queenstown, such as skiing, white water rafting, bungy jumping, jet boating, helicopter flights, adventure combination packages, mountain biking, horse riding and parachuting. The way to experience the best of these in one day is to do the 'awesome foursome.' You will start the day with the world's second highest bungy jump - the AJ Hackett Nevis - where you will catapult yourself off the end of what looks like a cable car, suspended between two mountains. This isn't for the faint-hearted, but promises an ultimate adrenaline rush. The rest of the day is pretty serene in comparison, although you will take a powerboat across the river, a helicopter ride, and whitewater raft down a river.

More leisurely activities include the historic TSS Earnslaw steamship, Walter Peak Station, the Skyline Gondola ride to the Skyline complex including restaurant, the exciting Luge ride and the entertaining 'Kiwi Magic'. There is also an excellent small vineyard - Chard Farm - between Queenstown and Arrowtown. They have an 'open cellar door policy' at this vineyard where you can taste their local specialities - such as Judge & Jury chardonnay.

Less than half an hour from Queenstown is Arrowtown, an historic gold-mining settlement. It's a real step back in time. It's a lovely place to visit, with an extraordinary outdoor museum describing the historic settlements of Chinese gold-mining immigrants. Try taking a private tour with one of the locals for a more personal insight to the area.

↵ Stylish Places to Stay

Grand Style: Blanket Bay. Opened in December 1999, this hotel heralded a new chapter in the history of luxury lodges in New Zealand. Situated at the northern end of Lake Wakatipu, it has a Swiss alpine lodge style. There are four intimate lakeside rooms and three sumptuous lodge suites.

Chic Boutique Style: The Spire. Seriously stylish and luxurious, this hotel's sleek cocktail bar is great to relax in after a hard day's activities. The Spire was nominated for four awards at The Annual World Travel Awards in 2007. A few years ago Queenstown needed a luxury boutique hotel, now they have a world leader on their doorstep! ☆

Country Style: Franz Josef Glacier Country Retreat. This hotel is set in 200 acres of peaceful family farmland, overlooks picturesque Lake Mapourika, and is only five minutes away from Franz Josef village. It's a perfect place to stay and explore the area. Rooms are 'modern country' style, and feature four-poster beds and loads of character.

⦿ Delicious Places to Eat

Seafood Style: Wai Waterfront restaurant. Specialising in seafood and Central Otago wines, this restaurant has a superb location on the waterfront of the Steamer Wharf. Try oysters with homemade bread and delicious dipping sauces.

Alfresco Dining: Beeches restaurant. Offering continental fine dining in Franz Josef, Beeches has a lovely outside dining area. Sit and stare at the amazing views of the glacier while sipping local wine. ☆

Members Only: The Bunker. This gem is discretely hidden down a dark alley in Queenstown with no signs or advertising. It's as exclusive as a member's bar, except your fellow drinkers are skiers not stockbrokers. Expect leather armchairs, log fires, and ambient music. Book for food, which is local eclectic cuisine.

Adventure: City Slicker
Destination: Christchurch -
Canterbury & Marlborough Region

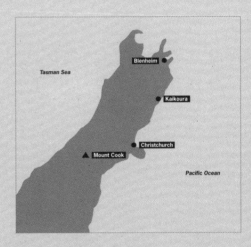

✈ Regional Information

Christchurch and the Marlborough region are two areas of the South Island that lovers of food, wine and nature cannot miss. The Southern Alps provide an impressive backdrop but Christchurch and Marlborough bask in year-round sunshine providing perfect conditions for hot-air ballooning, walking, sightseeing, sea-kayaking and wine tasting. It's a region where you can pick one of many themes and follow it through. Choose your itinerary from action adventure, vineyards and wineries, arts and crafts, or history and gardens. With so much variety, this region appeals to many types of travellers. You may want to spend a week or ten days exploring this region - if you can find the will power to leave the vineyards, that is!

Christchurch is a vibrant city with exciting festivals, innovative theatre, progressive art galleries, great shopping (including many international couture designers) and award winning attractions. It is the South Island's largest city and is renowned for its elegant grey stone 19th century buildings and its lush gardens. It is also known as 'the garden city'. Christchurch was originally planned to be a Church of England settlement and its founders intended that it should reflect English society. It certainly does that - it is reminiscent of old England about 50 years ago.

The town's flat land allowed for a grid of organised streets to be built bounded by wide tree-lined avenues. The distinctive stamp of English architecture has survived in its beautiful buildings, statues, parks and squares. This 130-year-old haven is the perfect place for a walk, or it can be enjoyed from a rowboat or a gentle punt down the meandering Avon River, which runs through the city centre.

The ever-popular International Antarctic Centre, located next to Christchurch's International Airport, is one of the main visitor attractions. Despite its unlikely location, it has entertaining and informative tours where visitors can don a warm woolly suit and experience sub-zero temperatures.

MONTANA
◄ BRANCOTT WINERY
RESTAURANT • WINE SALES

Adventure: City Slicker
Destination: Christchurch -

Canterbury & Marlborough Region

Another wonderful attraction is Orana Wildlife Park. The park is locally run and set in 80 hectares of grounds. It is New Zealand's only open-range zoo. You will love getting up close and personal by hand-feeding giraffes or petting calves and donkeys. During the spring you can see lambs being reared.

North of Christchurch is Hanmer Springs, an alpine spa at the base of the unspoiled Amuri mountain range. This picturesque township contains a relaxing thermal pool complex where temperatures range from 95-110°F (35-43°C). It's great for bathing away stress after sightseeing. You can hire a private area or bathe with the locals in the public areas. If you book in advance, you can also treat yourself to a massage.

Kaikoura, a small village north of Christchurch, is an impressive place where you can view the magnificent Giant Sperm Whale, as well as 200 other species of marine life in their natural habitat, including hundreds of fur seals sunbathing on a rocky shore and spectacular leaping dolphins. Whale-watching trips and swimming with the dolphins can be organised for you from the village. Tours operate all year from the Whaleway Station Road.

Methven, located in Central Canterbury, is New Zealand's finest ballooning location. Situated south west of Christchurch en-route to Queenstown, Aoraki Balloon Safaris will take you on a magical sky experience with great views of Mount Cook, the Southern Alps and a 300 km panorama of the Canterbury Plains. The flight concludes with a champagne-style breakfast.

Towards the north of the South Island are the intricate detail of the Marlborough Sounds, an extensive network of sea drowned valleys visible from the sea and from the air. Maori legend describes the entire South Island as Maui's waka (canoe), wrecked on a reef during a fishing expedition. The shattered bow of the canoe became the Sounds.

Wine tasting is a great experience in the South Island. The ever-popular wine trail is well established - it links various small and large wineries. The Marlborough Wine and Food Festival is held in February each year and attracts many visitors to sample Marlborough's produce while enjoying music and entertainment. The most popular vineyards to visit are Cloudy Bay, Montana and Herzog, which all tend to specialise in Sauvignon Blanc. All three of these vineyards will provide a small and informative tour plus wine-tasting opportunities.

Opposite page, from the top. Entrance of the George Hotel, Bedroom at the George Hotel, Sign of the Takahe.

↘ Stylish Places to Stay

Châteaux Chic: Châteaux Marlborough. This five star deluxe hotel is just a short walk from Blenheim centre. It offers a great base for exploring the nearby vineyards and has a relaxing and romantic feel. The hotel can also arrange trips up to Nelson (see Focus on Nelson on next page) and Kaikoura.

City Charm: The George. Located centrally in Christchurch, this lovely boutique hotel has recently won a Conde Nast's 'Gold List' award. Great views over Hagley Park and River Avon, and it's still only a short walk to the shopping district.

Country Style: Grasmere Lodge. Built in 1858, this traditional New Zealand lodge is full of character and charm. Great for outdoor adventurers, the hotel can arrange anything from sheep farming to clay-pigeon shooting! It is discreetly tucked away in the Southern Alps - perfect for those who really want to get away from it all.

🍽 Delicious Places to Eat

NZ Cuisine: Cook 'n' with Gas Bistro. This upbeat and quirky bistro has paper on the tables and NZ cuisine on the plates. An extensive beverage list (with over 40 domestic and international beers), and Beef & Lamb Ambassador 2006 welcomes customers. Located opposite the Court Theatre, the place is full of personality.

Wine & Dine: Pegasus Bay. This gorgeous winery in Waipara is only 45 minutes from Christchurch and has highly regarded wines and an award-winning restaurant. Free wine tastings are also available.

Royal class: Sign of the Takahe. This is regarded as one of the finest traditional dining experiences in New Zealand and is located in a heritage building with stunning views over Christchurch. Apparently prime ministers, ⭐ presidents and royalty dine here regularly.

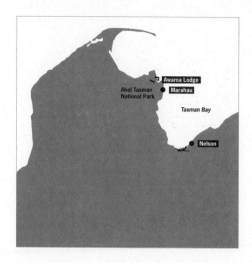

Focus On...
Abel Tasman National Park

The Abel Tasman National Park, located at the top of the South Island, is named after Dutch navigator Abel Tasman, who in 1642 became the first European explorer to sight New Zealand. At 22,530 hectares, Abel Tasman is New Zealand's smallest national park, but is renowned for its golden beaches, sculptured granite cliffs, and world-famous Abel Tasman Coast Track.

The region, which is the sunniest in New Zealand, has for many years attracted residents who love to use their imaginations. There are more than 350 working artists and craftspeople living in Nelson, including traditional and contemporary Maori artists. Their work is often inspired by the region's exceptionally beautiful geography - coastal, forest and valley landscapes - that provide places to wander and dream.

Abel Tasman National Park Experiences offer cruising, beach walks, and sea-kayaking through the spectacular Abel Tasman National Park. For serious hikers, the Nelson Lakes National Park displays the grandeur and beauty of the Nelson region. Day cruises and short easy walks are also available in the Abel Tasman National Park. The calm warm waters of the area provide safe swimming and sea kayaking with sea lions. One of the incredible sights to see from the sea is 'split apple rock' - an unusual rock formation. You can stay in a beachfront lodge in the park - one of the finest is Awaroa Lodge, with roaring fires, cosy luxurious rooms and direct access to the beach.

Opposite page. The Abel Tasman National Park.

(i) Stylish Essentials

General Information
www.newzealand.com/UK-Ireland
www.tourism.net.nz

Air New Zealand
www.airnewzealand.co.uk
T. 0800 028 4149 (UK only)

Qantas
www.qantas.co.uk
T. 0845 7 747 767 (UK Only)

Emirates
www.emirates.com/uk
T. 0870 243 2222 (UK Only)

Cathay Pacific
www.cathaypacific.com
T. 0208 834 8888 (UK Only)

Hire a campervan
www.britz.com
www.maui-rentals.com

The Cook Strait Crossing
www.interislander.co.nz

Luxury Coach Company
www.magicbus.co.nz

Northeast (Coromandel, Rotorua,
Wiakato, Lake Taupo)

Coromandel tourism Info
www.thecoromandel.com

Rotorua tourism info
www.rotorua.nz.com

Lake Taupo tourism Info
www.laketauponz.com

The Black water Rafting Company
www.waitomo.com/black-waterrafting.
aspx
T. +64 (07) 8786219

Hells Gate
www.hellsgate.co.nz
T. +64 (07) 345 3151

Tongariro Crossing Info
www.tongarirocrossing.org.nz

Huka Lodge
www.hukalodge.co.nz
T. +64 (07) 378 5791

Treetops Lodge
www.treetops.co.nz
T. +64 (07) 333 2066

Collieth Lodge
www.colleithlodge.co.nz
T. +64 (07) 864 7970

The Prawn Park
www.hukaprawnpark.co.nz
T. +64 (07) 374 8474

The Prawn Park
www.hukaprawnpark.co.nz
T. +64 (07) 374 8474

Admiral's restaurant
www.dineout.co.nz
T. +64 (07) 866 8020
Open: Winter 5pm until late, summer
11.00am-3.00pm, 5.00pm-late

Capers Epicurean
www.capers.co.nz
T. +64 (07) 348 8818
Open: 7.00am Monday to Friday and
7.30am Saturday and Sunday.
Tuesday to Saturday evenings for
night dining.

Southwest & Queenstown

General Information
www.west-coast.co.nz

TranzAlpine Train Journey
www.thetranzalpine.com

Heli-hike Franz Josef Glacier
www.franzjosefglacier.com/heli-hike.
html

TranzAlpine train
www.thetranzalpine.com

**Awesome Foursome inc AJ
Hackett Bungy**
www.everythingqueenstown.com/
item/55/Awesome+Foursome

Chard Farm
www.chardfarm.co.nz

Lord of the rings Tour
www.lordoftheringstours.co.nz

Blanket Bay
www.blanketbay.com
T. +64 (03) 441 0115

The Spire
www.thespirehotels.com
T. +64 (03) 441 0004

**Franz Josef Glacier Country
Retreat**
www.glacier-retreat.co.nz
T. +64 (03) 752 0012

Wai Waterfront Restaurant
T. +64 (03) 442 5969
www.wai.net.nz
Open: 7 Days a week from 6.00pm to
10.00pm. Lunch: December- March

Beeches Restaurant
T. +64 (03) 752 0721
Open: Dinner only

The Bunker Restaurant
www.thebunker.co.nz
T. +64 (03) 441 8030

Christchurch- Canterbury & Marlborough

General Information
www.christchurchnz.net

International Antarctic Centre
www.iceberg.co.nz
T. +64 (03) 353 7798
Open: Winter (April - September)
9.00am - 5.30pm, Summer
(October - March) 9.00am - 7.00pm

Orana Wildlife Park
www.oranawildlifepark.co.nz
T. +64 (03) 359 7109
Open: Daily 10.00am-5.00pm

Kaikoura Whale watching
www.whalewatch.co.nz
T. +64 (03) 319 6767

Hamner Springs
www.hanmersprings.co.nz
T. +64 (03) 315 0029
Open: Daily 10.00am-9.00pm

Aoraki Balloon Safaris
www.nzballooning.co.nz
T. +64 (03) 302 8172

Châteaux Marlborough
www.marlboroughnz.co.nz
T. +64 (03) 578 0064

The George
www.thegeorge.com
T. +64 (03) 379 4560

Grasmere Lodge
www.grasmere.co.nz
T. +64 (03) 318 8407

Cook 'n' with Gas Bistro
www.cooknwithgas.co.nz
T. +64 (03) 377 9166
Open: Mon-Sat evenings only

Pegasus Bay
www.pegasusbay.com
T. +64 (03) 314 6869
Open: Wine tastings and sales from
10.30am to 5.00pm seven days.
Restaurant is open from 12.00 noon
to 4.00 pm every day.

Sign of the Takahe
www.signofthetakahe.co.nz
T. +64 (03) 332 4052
Open: Call for more information

Nelson - Abel Tasman National Park

General Information
www.abeltasmaninformation.co.nz

Sea Kayaking
www.marahauseakayaks.co.nz
T. +64 (03) 527 8551

Sea shuttle / Day excursions
www.abeltasmanseashuttles.co.nz
T. +64 (03) 528 9759

Awaroa Lodge
www.awaroalodge.co.nz
T. +64 (03) 528 8758

View from the Bund, Shanghai

CHINA

Beijing | Shanghai | Chengdu | Xi'an

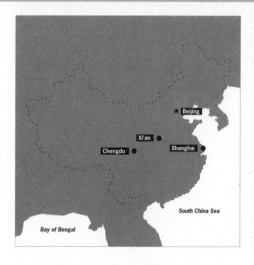

Why is this place so special?

China is a land beyond all preconceived ideas, a land surrounding lush tropical rainforests, towering snow-covered mountains, roaring rivers and wild rapids. There are so many things to explore throughout this vast land - from the snowcaps of the Himalayas to the sweep of the Yangtze River, and from the slick city of Shanghai to the tribal hills of the Southwest. The continuing thread is the human landscape, the ordinary Chinese people - their friendliness, hospitality and curiosity is an attraction in itself. Rural China offers a land of breathtaking rice terraces, unspoiled villages and placid lakes, all of which can really soothe the soul. At the same time, modern day China is a land of skyscraping cities, extraordinary shopping, luxury hotels and wonderful restaurants.

China is one of the world's oldest civilisations. It boasts some of the most admired treasures - such as temples, pagodas and Buddhist statues - which speak of history, contemplation and culture. China has 31 UNESCO world heritage sites, including the 6,700 km Great Wall and the Mausoleum of the First Qin Emperor, also known as the Terracotta Warriors, entombed for centuries with the First Emperor.

China is also a shopper's delight. There is an incredible selection of boutique shops and department stores, as well as bargain hunting at any of the new 'free markets' which have sprung up all over the country. Throughout China, shops offer local ceramics, paintings, jade carvings, custom-carved signature chopsticks, high-quality silks, antique screens and traditional herbal medicines. With so much choice it is hard to know what to buy!

Shanghai is home to some 14 million people and is one of China's largest and most cosmopolitan cities. Overlooking the Huangpu River, it is a beautiful city mixing traditional Chinese and 21st century architecture. At night, the city comes alive on the Bund, where lights illuminate highways, buildings and the Huangpu River.

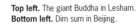

Top left. The giant Buddha in Lesham.
Bottom left. Dim sum in Beijing.

Few people take their food as seriously as the Chinese. Authentic Chinese food is delectable, and with 56 ethnic groups contributing to recipes cultivated over centuries, it's no wonder there is so much choice and variety. Every traveller should make sure they sample some of the local and regional cuisine that each area has to offer.

Whether your notion of adventure is discovering an ancient civilisation, hiking the mountains, taking a slow boat on a long river, or dining on 5,000 years of gastronomic experience, modern-day China has a lot to offer. We recommend a stay of at least three weeks in order to fully explore the country's highlights.

Fast Facts

Capital: Beijing

Location: China is situated in Eastern Asia on the coast of the Pacific Ocean. It covers an area of 9.6 million sq km.

Population: China is the world's most populous country. It has more than 1.2 billion inhabitants - almost a fifth of the world's total. To bring population growth under control, the country has followed a family planning policy since the 1970s.

Religion: China is a multi-religious country, where Taoism, Buddhism, Islam and Christianity are practised.

Language: Mandarin is commonly used in modern China. The majority of the 55 other ethnic groups have their own languages. There are also many dialects around the country. As a written language, Chinese has been used for 6,000 years.

Getting there and exploring around

Getting to China by air is relatively easy. Travellers can fly directly into Hong Kong from the UK with Cathay Pacific, BA or Virgin Atlantic. Air China also flies directly to Beijing and Shanghai from the UK. Air Canada and Air China are the two major carriers from Canada. Some passengers take flights via the USA by United Airlines or Northwest Airlines, or they take flights via Hong Kong, Tokyo and Seoul by Cathay Pacific, Japan Airlines, or Korean Airlines.

It is also relatively easy to enter China by rail from Europe or Asia. Popular routes from Europe are the Trans-Siberian Express (from Moscow), or the Trans-Mongolian Express from St Petersburg to Beijing. From Asia, you can take a train from Vietnam to Beijing, from Kowloon to Beijing or from Kowloon to Shanghai.

There are also options for travelling by water. Ferry services run from from Japan or South Korea into various major Chinese ports, including Shanghai, Tianjin (Tanggu), Dalian, Hong Kong and Macao.

Once you're inside China, you have a number of options to explore the country. Internal flights are reasonably cheap, and reliable, although the general standards of cleanliness are not like those in the West.

Travelling across China by rail affords you the greatest opportunity to see the breadth of this vast country and is an enjoyable and inexpensive experience. Many of China's trains have first-class compartments. New or modernised equipment has replaced old trains in many areas. Travellers who lack the time to cover long distances by train can still get a delightful taste of rail travel by journeying on popular short-distance routes. Examples of journey times include: 28 hours from Hong Kong to Beijing; 15 hours from Shanghai to Beijing; 14 hours from Xi'an to Beijing; 2 hours from Shanghai to Hangzhou, and 45 minutes from Shanghai to Suzhou.

Buses are another excellent option. With the development over the last decade of a national highway system, luxurious coaches have become an increasingly popular mode of transportation for tourists.

Taxis are available in all of China's major cities. Always carry your hotel card with you and ask the hotel concierge to write down the address of your destination in Chinese characters. Although most taxi drivers speak English in larger cities - like Beijing, Shanghai and Guangzhou - many in other cities may not understand the language.

Bicycles are available for rent throughout China, although with nine million bicycles in Beijing alone, it's a fairly ambitious way to get around.

Despite the availability of all these options to explore China independently, the easiest and quickest way to see China's main attractions is to use a private tour group.

☞ Best time of year to visit

China is characterised by a continental climate. The latitudes span nearly 50 degrees; the south is in the tropical and subtropical zones, while the north is near the frigid zones.

Spring (March to April) and Autumn (September to October) are the best times to visit, though the higher altitude areas of Tibet, Qinghai and Western Sichuan are best visited in high Summer (June to September). Daytime temperatures range from 20-30°C (68-86°F) during these seasons, but nights can get bitterly cold and can sometimes be wet and miserable. Major public holidays, in particular Chinese New Year, are best avoided, as it can be difficult to get around or find accommodation.

The best months to visit Beijing are May, June, September and October. The climate in early Spring may not be good, because you might meet 'yellow storms' (seasonal dust storms). Autumn is the best season to visit Beijing because you will more than likely get blue skies. If you're visiting during January it might even snow!

? Must know before you go

Be wary of what you buy. Avoid buying anything if you are unsure of its origin. The trade of illegal animal products is the most acute in Asia. Many poachers slaughter endangered animals to provide souvenirs for tourists. The killing of these animals will stop when the buying stops. Ask about a product's origin before you buy.
Avoid the spitting. Locals spit everywhere - on the street, in taxis and even on planes. Make sure you watch out for flying spit and wash your hands before eating to avoid the 'Shanghai Flu.' The government is trying to crack down on spitting, and supposedly taxis are now being equipped with spitting sacks for passengers and drivers.
Take a picture dictionary. The majority of Chinese do not speak English, and in international chains of hotels, tourist areas and cities, their command of English can be very basic. Even if you learn greetings in Mandarin, it can still be a struggle to communicate. The easiest way to get by is to produce your own 'picture dictionary', which consists of a set of pictures of important words and phrases. This way you can point to the things you are trying to say, rather than attempt to explain them verbally. Also, remember to always carry the business card of where you are staying when you are out and about.

📖 Highlights

The Great Wall of China. The wall is one of the Seven Wonders of the World and is UNESCO listed. The scenery can be enjoyed from many of the restored sections. If you have more time, visit a section which has not been restored - not to be missed!
Chengdu Giant Panda Research Base. Learn about these incredible gentle animals and stroll around the vast park grounds to experience them in their natural habitat.
Dim Sum and Shopping in Shanghai. Explore one of the world's most fascinating cities, get a tailor-made suit in 24 hours, buy some ornate chopsticks or feast on delicious dim-sum.
Big Buddha in Leshan. Poised on a cliff and carved out of stone, the Big Buddha is a masterpiece. Reaching 71 metres high, the imposing and commanding Buddha can be seen from miles around.

Adventure: Culture Vulture
Destination: Beijing

✦ Regional Information

Beijing, the country's capital, is a bustling city with more than ten million people. It is home to an incredible display of cultural and historical artifacts in more than 50 museums. Other cultural attractions include folk traditions in theatres, delicious dining in exotic settings, and cultural centres which offer fascinating demonstrations of centuries old art and craft making. Modern day Beijing represents the heart of China's political, economic, cultural and educational affairs and is the nation's most important hub for international trade and communications

On the one hand, the city has been the heart and soul of China's society as a whole throughout its long history. Consequently, it offers unparalleled cultural riches to delight and intrigue travellers as they explore its royal past and enjoy its exciting modern development. China's two final dynasties (1368-1911) and its 26 emperors bestowed Beijing with a dynastic heritage which dates back more than 3,000 years.

On the other hand, the city has entered the 21st century with a brand new image, while maintaining a number of traditional characterstics. It is a must for anyone who loves culture. If you are prepared to travel outside the city walls then you can also enjoy breathtaking scenery. We recommend that you allow at least five days to explore this magnificent city.

One of the most important attractions is the Forbidden City, which lies in the heart of the city and is gated by Tiananmen Square. Built in 1406 during the Ming dynasty, the city is actually a city within a city. It has 9,999 rooms and covers 720,000 square meters. During the Ming and Qing dynasty, 24 emperors made their home in the Forbidden City and forbade commoners from entering. Today, the Emperor's Palace has been transformed into a museum which holds many treasures of the Imperial Family. Puyi, the last Emperor, occupied the Inner Palace as a royal residence until 1924.

Adventure: Culture Vulture
Destination: Beijing

The Summer Palace, built in 1750, overlooks tranquil Kunming Lake. It used to be a Summer holiday home for Chinese royalty. Strolling along the palace's corridors allows you to imagine the palace in action.

The Ming dynasty tombs are not to be missed. They are located 50 km north of Beijin. Large stone animals and human figures line the sacred way to the entrance to the imperial burial ground - a complex of tombs of 13 emperors from the Ming dynasty.

The Great Wall of China must be top of your agenda in China. When you first look at the Great Wall it is impossible not to be awestruck at this man-made structure. Although some parts have now been restored there are still some areas off the beaten track which have not been restored. These parts of the wall are extremely rewarding, although you will need to put do your own research if you want to locate them.

Construction of the wall started in the 7th century BC, with additions and rebuilding continuing until the 16th century AD. The Great Wall was built to keep out the warring invaders of the North, but additional sections were extended eastwards for nearly 6,700 km. The most popular restored sections are Mutianyu and Badaling, which are within a day's trip from Beijing city. These sections attract millions of tourists every year. That said, to get the best out of any visit, stay near the Great Wall the night before (preferably two nights) and beat the early morning crowds.

Street sellers line up to sell to tourists, so you can pick up any number of tourist souvenirs. But the best place to see talented local artists is at the Cloisonné factory near Mutianyu, where you can watch them at work.

Cloisonné is a unusual combination of copper and porcelain working skills, traditional painting, sculpting and etching skills; it can take weeks of layering to produce even something small. This factory also has an excellent shop. If you have a tour guide, it will normally include a visit to this factory - or you can go independently.

Although Beijing is a modern and fashionable city, with 21st century vitality, you can experience 'old Beijing' by exploring its many tea-houses, temple fairs and the Peking Opera. The Peking Opera, which originated in the late 18th century, is a synthesis of music, dance, art and acrobatics. It is the most influential and representative of all the operas in China. The operas can be divided into 'civil' pieces and 'martial' pieces. Civil pieces are characterised by singing and 'martial' ones feature acrobatics and stunts. Some operas are a combination of both. See Stylish Essentials for more details.

↩ Stylish Places to Stay

Ranch Style: Red Capital Ranch. Hidden miles away from the bustling city and smog of Beijing, the Great Wall is so close to your room you can see un-restored sections of the wall, and can walk up it unguided within an hour. Each room (or chalet) is individually styled; the whole place has a unique feeling of calm and tranquillity. Breakfast is usually included in the price and the food is an eclectic mix of Mongolian, Tibetan and Chinese cuisine. We can't recommend this place highly enough. There is also a sister hotel 'Red Capital Club' in Beijing city. ☆

Designer Style: The Commune on the Great Wall. This is a real find, but must be booked way in advance. It is a luxury hideaway with wonderfully individually designed suites which reflect the price tag. Each 'commune' has been created by design masters around the world. Although it recently has been taken over by German chain 'Kempinski' it hasn't lost any of its appeal and exclusivity.

Skyline Style: China World Hotel. The 2003 renovations sent this hotel soaring above all others in Beijing. From the outside it looks oddly like a convex version of the UN building. The design is sophisticated and the luxury touches are well considered. Large modern beds greet your body like a warm embrace, and the spacious marble bathrooms pamper you with high-end toiletries.

⊙ Delicious Places to Eat

Tibetan Cuisine: Red Capital Ranch. This Manchurian style lodge is located near the Great Wall and has beautifully carved tables and decorations. It serves locally prepared Chinese cuisine with a Tibetan twist. The view of the river is awesome, as is the service. Try drinking the yak's milks with frozen yak meat. ☆

Beijing Duck: Lichun Kaoyadian. Located down the alleyways of the Hutong district, this restaurant serves superbly presented food which is prepared to a high standard.

Northern Delights: Made in China. Located at the Grand Hyatt Hotel in Beijing, this place specialises in fantastic northern Chinese cuisine. It features flaming apricot-wood-fired ovens and a bustling atmosphere. It's fairly new but has developed a loyal client base, and is popular with the locals. You can't go wrong!

Adventure: City Slicker
Destination: Shanghai

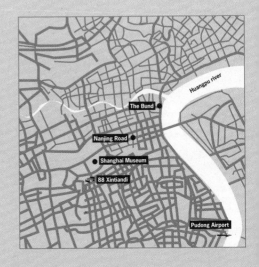

✦ Regional Information

Overlooking the Huangpu River, Shanghai is home to 14 million people and is one of China's largest and most cosmopolitan cities. It is a beautiful city, mixing traditional Chinese and 21st century architecture. At night, the city comes alive with lights which line highways, buildings, the famous 'Bund' and the Huangpu River. Long ago, Shanghai was originally a tiny fishing village but today it is a dazzling city swirling with rapid cultural change. A couple of days here should be enough to browse the city's highlights.

Since the first half of the 20th century Shanghai has developed into China's largest commercial city. Today, over 300 of the world's top 500 enterprises have branches in Shanghai. Lujiazui in Pudong has also become one of the top financial and trade zones in Asia. Landmark constructions and skyscrapers emerge one after another, such as the Oriental Pearl TV Tower, Jin Mao Tower, and Shanghai International Convention Center. These remarkable buildings are especially alluring at night when they light up the skyline. Shanghai has many attractions in the downtown region, including the Huangpu River, the Bund, the Shanghai Museum and the Yuyuan Garden.

The Huangpu River joins Shanghai just north of downtown Shanghai and divides the city into two parts, East and West. Cruises are available every day and you can choose from a short cruise - which navigates the main waterfront area between the Yangpu Bridge and the Nanpu Bridge - and a long cruise, which takes you eastwards over a distance of 60 km (37 miles). Tour boats leave from the dock on the Bund. The Huangpu River offers some remarkable views of the Bund and the activity on the riverfront.

The Bund, also called the Zhongshan Road, is a famous waterfront and has been regarded as the symbol of Shanghai for hundreds of years. It starts from the Baidu Bridge - which is at the connecting point of the Huangpu River and the Suzhou Creek - to the East Jinling Road. The Bund is on the west coast of the Huangpu River and is 1,500 meters (less than one mile) in length. As you walk along the Bund, look out for the Oriental Pearl TV Tower and the Jin Mao Tower on the opposite side of the river. The Bund is a beautiful and special place and is well worth visiting.

Shanghai is a shopper's paradise. The city's close proximity to some of the world's largest textile manufacturers makes this city an excellent place to buy value-for-money fashion clothing and accessories. Since market restrictions have lifted, and since the Shanghainese began paying particular attention to consumer tastes and material benefits, Shanghai has become a bit of a showcase for fashion, both domestically and internationally. Innovation and sophistication have taken over the city's retail areas. Retail shops litter every corner of the city, especially on Nanjing Road, Huaihai Road, North Sichuan Road (Hongkou district) and in Xujiahui (Xujia district).

Nanjing Road (Huangpu & Jingan district) was the first shopping street in China, and it is generally the busiest. In fact, it is so busy that the entire road has been pedestrianised. Nanjing Road has more than 600 shops, many of which are international retailers, such as Zara, Omega, L'Occitane and Lacoste, which sell local crafts, textiles, clothing, among other goods. It's worth visiting the Yunhong chopstick shop, where you can find hundreds of different styles of hand-made chopsticks. Also, head to Silk King to buy a tailor made silk suit - they can make one up within 24 hours.

Huaihai Road (Luwan & Xuhui district) is another street which is famous for shopping. The street boasts some 400 stores which mainly sell high and medium end goods. There are many shops and boutiques which offer well known brands of garments and footwear. Times Square on Huaihai Road is home to many internationally recognised brands (such as Gucci), the exclusive retailer Lane Crawford, as well as other popular stores like Esprit.

The shops on North Sichuan Road (Hongkou district) sell a large assortment of daily necessities which are made mainly in China and that have prices which are suitable for those who like to get good value for money.

Xujiahui (Xujia district) contains a cluster of large shopping malls in which you can buy almost everything - from clothes to computer gadgets. Head to the Pacific Digital Plaza for digital gadgets at bargain prices, but be watchful for fake imported goods!

Yuyuan Commercial City (Nanshi district) is known locally as the 'Kingdom of Shanghai Arts & Crafts and Small Articles'. It sells a whole range of articles, including antiques, precious stones, gold and silver products, jewellery, bottle caps and silk threads.

The Yu Garden, south of the Nanji Theng Road, offers a great respite from the hustle and bustle of the city - it could be described as 'the lungs of the city'. It was built in 1559, during the Ming dynasty, and has an exquisite layout and is a vision of greenery.

Adventure: City Slicker
Destination: Shanghai

As far as food is concerned, Shanghai enjoys an international reputation for excellent cuisine with a huge choice of speciality dishes. You can choose from a wide range of dining options in some of the finest restaurants in China. Or, you can opt to eat on the streets from one of the many vendors who seem to instantly appear at meal times. Shanghai food is influenced by its surrounding provinces and is often sweeter than you think. It is big on preserved vegetables, pickles, salted meats and strong flavours.

That said, by far the best food is dim sum - freshly steamed buns with a variety of savoury and sweet fillings served in a bamboo box. Dim sum translates literally as 'dot heart', or more poetically as 'little favourite close to the heart'. There is nowhere better to eat these 'dollops of delight' than in Old Shanghai, a maze of narrow lanes south of the Bund and the Huangpu river. Also, try the deep fried dumplings off the Holloway Road - buns, dumplings and rice rolls stuffed with fresh ingredients and served with lashings of tea.

Shanghai boasts a rich nightlife. To see its spectacular skyline by night, take an evening cruise around the harbour (see earlier section on Huangpu River) or head out to one of the theatres, operas, discos, acrobat shows, karaoke clubs or upscale lounges. If you like to go shopping at night, you can bargain to your heart's content in one of the designer boutiques which are open day and night along Nanjing Road.

If you want to spend your evening drinking in a bar, the best place to head is the Bund. Many bars have views of the skyline from rooftop lounges and VIP areas. Some even have sandy beaches. One of the best bars along the Bund is Bund 18, where they spark-up the bar with lighter fluid, to create a dancing flame. Just watch your eyebrows!

If you find that the sightseeing, clubbing and eating has worn you out, relax your mind and stretch your body by experiencing the ancient martial art of Tai Chi. The Chinese characters for Tai Chi can be translated as the 'supreme ultimate force'. Tai Chi, as it is practised in the West today, can perhaps best be thought of as a moving form of yoga and meditation. There are a number of forms - or 'sets' - which consist of a sequence of movements. Many of these movements are originally derived from martial arts, although in Tai Chi they are performed slowly, softly and gracefully with smooth and even transitions between them. Another aim of Tai Chi is to foster a calm and tranquil mind, which is achieved by focusing the mind on the precise execution of these exercises. Many practitioners notice benefits in terms of correcting poor postural alignment or patterns of movement, which can be caused by tension and can result in pain, or even injury. Furthermore, the meditative nature of the exercises is calming and relaxing itself. There are a couple of centres in Shanghai where visitors can experience Tai Chi and join a class. If you just want to be a spectator, then watch the locals starting their day with Tai Chi in the many parks in the morning. Fuxing Park (also known locally as French Park) is one of the loveliest green spots to watch Tai Chi. There is also an academy in Shanghai if you want to participate - they run classes on weekdays and at weekends (see Stylish Essentials for details).

⤴ Stylish Places to Stay

Apartment Chic: 88 Xintiandi. Located in the French Quarter opposite Fuxing park, this place is a lovely alternative to the high rise skyscraper hotels in the business district. The rooms are spacious with kitchenettes, full sized dressing areas, luxury bathrooms and Juliet balconies overlooking the park. They also deliver fresh fruit to your room every day.

Secluded Style: Fuchun Resort. Designed by Aman Resorts Veteran Jean-Michel Gathy, this hotel is rural and secluded. It is surrounded by wooded hillsides and is set against the backdrop of the Fuchun mountains. Located just outside of Hangzhou, 150 miles from Shanghai, the resort was inspired by a classic Chinese landscape painting, the 14th century Dwelling in the Fuchun Mountains. This place is a great retreat from the big city. ⭐

French Villa Style: Mansion Boutique Hotel. Developed 70 years ago, this hotel was once the former headquarters for gangster Du Yuesheng. Now, it's partly a museum and partly a luxury boutique hotel with 32 rooms. The Mansion's rooftop has been renovated into a bar, which looks out over the low rooftops of the French Concession. It feels very much like a clubhouse.

⦿ Delicious Places to Eat

Stylish Cuisine: M on the Bund. With Art Deco style elegance, M boasts a terrace with unsurpassed views of the Bund, the Huangpu River, and Pudong's skyscrapers. It also has a Glamour Room for nightly dinner and drinks. Open for a lazy lunch or glam it up for dinner. ⭐

Dim Sum Delight: Nanxiang. Located in the centre of the old town, this place is a must for dim sum. They serve every variety of you can imagine and every single one is homemade. The restaurant was founded in 1900 and is an institution in Shanghai.

Chinese Fusion: T8 Shanghai. Set in the elegant and ultra-hip shopping and dining district of Xintiandi, T8 is located down a narrow alleyway which runs between 19th century buildings made from stone and brick. You enter on a slate path set over fish-filled ponds and take your place at a cosy cocktail bar. The open plan kitchen and dining area is decorated with dark lacquered furniture in warm Asian tones. The food is a sexy Mediterranean and Asian fusion brought to you by an award-winning Australian chef. The fabulous wine list, dominated by the New World, is the best in the city. Great drinks, design, décor and dining - T8 is not to be missed.

Opposite page. Pandas at the research centre.

Adventure: Nature Lover
Destination: Chengdu
& Leshan

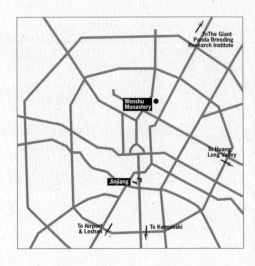

✦ Regional Information

Chengdu is the capital of the Sichuan province, or 'Heavenly State' (Tian Fu Zhi Guo), habitat of giant pandas. The city is located in the west of Sichuan Basin and is in the centre of the fertile Chengdu Plain. Chengdu's history can be traced back 2,400 years when the first emperor built his capital here and named the city. Chengdu is one of China's most important economic centres. To explore the region, we would recommend you spend at least three days in the area.

The city holds a number of important historical accolades. More than 4,000 years ago, the prehistoric bronze age culture is believed to have established itself in this region. Also, Chengdu is the place where the Southern Silk Road started, as well as being the place where the earliest paper currency, Jiaozi, was first printed.

In addition to its profound historical and cultural background, the city features many historic places of interest, such as the Wuhou Memorial Temple and the Wenshu Monastery. It also boasts natural beauty in its surrounding areas, such as in the Jiuzhaigou Scenic Area and Huang Long Valley (Yellow Dragon Valley).

The most interesting attractions in the region include the Chengdu Panda Research Centre and the Wolong Breeding Centre. The Wolong Breeding Centre and the Chengdu Research Base are probably the two best-known panda breeding facilities in the country and have been very successful at producing cubs. The Chengdu Research Base for giant panda breeding is located just outside the huge metropolis of Chengdu, but the Wolong Breeding Centre is much further afield. Both facilities were established for wildlife and habitat conservation purposes, not as a tourist attraction, so there isn't a lot of information available or tours to the areas. Your best option is to get a taxi from Chengdu to the Chengdu Research Base, or to plan a two-day trip to Wolong Breeding Centre and stay at a local hotel in Wolong village.

Giant Pandas are one of the world's best known endangered animals. There are only about one thousand left in the wild. The rare animal is endemic to China, though some of the habitats were found in Northern Vietnam and other nearby areas over half a million years ago. They are known for their low reproductive rates, which is partly one of the reasons why the number of animals in the wild is declining.

At the Chengdu Research Base, you can observe adult pandas and baby pandas playing and eating (which they like to do best). But few people know that you can make a donation to the organisation and have a close-up encounter. Being so close to these lovable creatures is a wonderful experience. They have spiky fur and their playful manner and unusual black markings make them so adorable. The encounter is not publicised so you need to ask one of the wardens. The base is a huge, beautifully landscaped park, and there are plenty of opportunities to spot the pandas playing or sleeping without being disturbed by tourists.

There are other natural formations and scenic attractions in the area, such as Huanglong Valley. This valley was made a UNESCO world natural heritage site in 1992. Huanglong wins its fame for its magical landscape of limestone formations and 3,400 multi-coloured ponds paved with golden calcite deposits. The valley also boasts wonderful waterfalls, stalactite caves and three ancient temples. At the end of the valley, water from melting snow envelopes limestone formations from underground, and flows down the mountain terraces depositing calcium carbonate from the limestone on the rocks, stones, and fallen branches in its path. You could spend whole day just walking here and marvelling at the scenery.

Adventure: Nature Lover
Destination: Chengdu
& Leshan

Outside Chengdu lays the impressive Giant Buddha in Leshan, one of the area's main highlights. The Giant Buddha looks out on to the confluence of three rivers - the Min River, Qingyi River, and Dadu River - and is a scenic and cultural wonder. At 71 metres tall, it is the largest Buddha in the world (its fingers are 3 metres long). The Buddha was included by UNESCO on the list of the World Heritage sites in December 1996. Construction of the Buddha is believed to have begun in 713 AD during the Tang Dynasty and it was completed in 803 AD - making a total of 90 years!

After years of erosion by wind and rain, the Buddha was restored and repaired in 1963 by the Chinese government. Today, maintenance work is still carried out under the instruction of experts from UNESCO. The Buddha is a stone-carved statue of Maitreya (a Bodhisattva, or someone who seeks enlightenment, represented as a very stout monk in sitting posture with a broad smile on his face and with his naked breast and paunch exposed to view). The statue makes itself one of the most renowned scenic spots in Leshan City. You can climb up to the top and wander around the head, or queue to climb down beneath the feet (which will take a few hours). It's worth taking a 15-minute boat trip from the nearby dock to view the Buddha from the river.
From this angle you can see the Buddha in its entirety and it's a great photo opportunity.

The Buddha is located to the East of Leshan City. It isn't an easy place to reach from Chengdu City, but it can be done in a day. A taxi drive will take about two hours from Chengdu centre. If you are staying in Leshan you can catch a ferry from Yibin City, Luzhaou City or Chongqing City to Leshan Port. You can also get the train from Chengdu and get off at Emei station. This station is 10 km (about six miles) away from the gate of Mount. Emei, and 31 km (about 19 miles) away from Leshan City.

↘ Stylish Places to Stay

City Style: Kempinski. Mainly catering for business travellers, this is a beautiful hotel with lovely and comfortable rooms. The bathrooms are gorgeous. The spa has exclusive massages and the pool is like a hot tub. Perfect to soak those limbs after a day's sightseeing.

Deco Style: Jin Jiang Hotel. The Shanghai Jin Jiang Hotel has two gardens and three European-style buildings with art-deco interiors and friendly staff. Great location and a buffet breakfast serving an excellent variety of Western and Chinese food.

Oriental Style: Samsara Hotel. This hotel is reasonably priced and has a good location with oriental style interiors. There is a fabulous rooftop pool on the 9th floor and helpful concierge service to help you plan any last minute excursions.

🍽 Delicious Places to Eat

Vegetarian delights: Wenshu Temple Restaurant. For the vegetarian palette, this place is an absolute must. The realistic tasting prawns and sausages made of tofu will fool even the most bloodthirsty of carnivores. The temple is a beautiful setting for this unique eatery. ⭐

Sichuan sizzle: Gingko. This is one of the few restaurants in Sichuan where you'll feel out of place unless you dress up to dine. It mainly serves Cantonese and Sichuan styles of cuisine. Try the king crab with peppercorns.

Local cuisine: Baguo Buyi. This restaurant offersfresh natural ingredients with some local and regional delicacies. Some dishes may not be to everyone's taste. But if you enjoy experimenting with food then this is the place for you. Food is served in a lovely rustic environment with spiral wooden staircases.

Focus On...
Terra Cotta Warriors in Xi'an

Just one-and-a-half hours by air from Beijing, Xi'an city is home to the world famous Terracotta Army, one of the greatest archaeological discoveries in the world.

Unearthed in 1974 (by a farmer who was digging a well), the discovery had been buried with the emperor Qin Shihuang for 22 centuries. The Terracotta Army is housed in three exhibition halls (the largest being 180 metres by 60 metres). It consists of over 6,000 terracotta soldiers and horses that once guared the tomb of Qin Shihuang, the first emperor of unified China. The terracotta figures are life-like and life-sized, and vary in height, uniform and hairstyle in accordance with rank. Each figure has unique facial features and expressions.

The horsemen are shown wearing tight-sleeved outer robes, short coats of chainmail and wind-proof caps. The archers also have bodies and limbs positioned in strict accordance with an ancient book on the art of war.

It is a stunning exhibition of ancient artefacts that is well laid out, easy to view and navigate around - although it can become a little overcrowded during peak season with bus loads of tourists.

There is a very helpful museum on site, which has an enclosure where you can listen to the story of the Terracotta Army in more detail, aswell as buy an array of gifts from the well-stocked shop.

Xi'an was the essence of the ancient Chinese civilisation dating back to 4,000 BC. It was the former capital of China for 11 dynasties up to the 9th century. It is still the capital of the Shaanxi Province today. The massive city wall and moat that still surround the city are a monument to its past glories.

Today, modern hotels complement a rich cultural heritage that invites exploration of the Shaanxi Province. Getting to Xi'an is easy, the main airport has direct flights from Beijing and Chengdu. The Terracotta Army is a drive away from the main airport (roughly 30 minutes) so you could actually visit it in a day, or stay over night to explore the area a bit further.

Opposite page. Terracotta Warriors in line.

ⓘ Stylish Essentials

China Tourism Info
www.cnto.org

British Embassy in Beijing
www.uk.cn

Chinese Embassy in UK
www.chinese-embassy.org.uk/eng

Cathay Pacific
www.cathaypacific.com
T. 0208 834 8888 (UK reservations)

British Airways
www.ba.com
T. 0870 850 9850 (UK reservations)

Virgin Atlantic
www.virgin-atlantic.com
T. 0870 380 2007 (UK reservations)

Air China
www.airchina.com.cn
T. 0207 744 0800 (UK reservations)

Air Canada
www.aircanada.ca
T. 0871 220 1111 (UK reservations)

Trans Siberian Express & Trans-Mongolian Express
www.expresstorussia.com
T. 0207 100 7370
(UK General enquiries)

China National Rail System
www.seat61.com/China.htm

Beijing

General Info
www.beijinghighlights.com/cityguide/general.htm

Beijing Capital International Airport
http://en.bcia.com.cn
T. +86 (0) 10-64541100
(Airport inquiries only)

Great wall of China
www.thebeijingguide.com/great_wall_of_china/index.html

Peking Opera House
Haihu West lane, No30,
Fengtai District, Beijing
T. +86 (0) 1067 227775

Laoshe Teahouse
No. 3 Qiannenxi Dajie Street, (Near south Side of Tianaman Square),
Beijing
www.laosheteahouse.com
(Chinese only)
T. +86 (0)10 6304 6334

Red Capital Ranch & Club
www.redcapitalclub.com.cn
T. +86 (0)10 8401 8886

Commune On the Great Wall
www.communebythegreatwall.com/en
T. +86 (0)10 81181888

China World Hotel
www.shangri-la.com/ChinaWorld
T. +86 (0)10 6505 2266

Made in China
www.beijing-hyatt.com
T. +86 (0)10 85181234
Open: Lunch and dinner

Lichun Kaoyadian
Lichun Kaoyadian Beixianfeng Hutong
T. +86 (0)10 6552 8310
Open: Dinner only

Shanghai

General Info
www.shanghai.city-tourist-information.com

Shanghai Pudong International Airport
www.shanghaiairport.com
T. +86 (0)21 6834 1000

General Shopping Information
www.china.org.cn/english/travel/104122.htm

Jin Mao Tower
Luijiazui Lu
www.jinmao88.com
T. +86 (0)21 5047 5101 (info)
Open: viewing platform:
8.30 am – 9.00 pm

Shanghai Museum of Arts and Crafts
Fenyang Lu 79
T. +86 (0)21 6327 2829 (info)
Open: Daily 8.30 am – 4.30 pm

Huangpu River Cruise
219-239 Zhongshan Dong Erlu
www.pjrivercruise.com
T. +86 (0)21 6374 4461 (info)
E. rivercruise@pjrivercruise.com
Open: 9.30 am – 9.00 pm

Yuyuan Garden
218 Anren Jie 200010
www.yuyuantm.com.cn
T. +86 (0)21 6355 5025 (info)
Open: 8.30 am – 5.00 pm
Admission Price: CNY 40

Silk King
66 Nanjing Road, Shanghai China

Yunhong Chopsticks Shop
387 East Nanjing Rd
T. +86 (0)21 6322 0207 (info)

Times Square
No.99, Huaihai Road M.
(near Longmen Road)
www.shtimessquare.com/shopping/index.htm
T. +86 (0)21 63910314
Open: 10:00-22:00

Pacific Digital Plaza
No.1119, Zhaojiabang Road near Caoxi Road N.
T. +86 (0)21 54905900

Tai Chi Academy
Wu's Tai Chi Chuan Academy,
No5 Lane 1295, Fuxing Road
T. +86 (0)21 64334084
www.wutaichi.com

Fuxing Park
Located on Nanchang Lu
Open: Daily 6.00 am – 6.00 pm

88 Xintiandi
www.88xintiandi.com
T. +86 (0)21 5383 8833

Mansion Boutique Hotel
www.chinamansionhotel.com
T.+86 (0)21 5403 9888

Fuchun Resort
www.fuchunresort.com/cn
T. +86 571 6346 1111

M on the Bund
www.m-onthebund.com
T. +86 (0)21 6350 9988

**Nanxiang Steaned Buns
Restaurant**
85 Yu Yuan Rd Old Town
T. +86 (0)21 6355 4206

T8 Shanghai
www.t8shanghai.com
T. +86 (0)21 6355 8999

Chengdu & Leshan

**Chengdu Suhangliu
International Airport**
www.cdairport.com

**Wolong Giant Panda
Breeding Centre**
Sichuen, China
www.ahfan.com/wolong/

**Chengdu Panda Research
Base**
www.panda.org.cn/english/
eindex.htm
T. +86 (0)28 83516748
E. pandaivf@mail.sc.cninfo.net

The Giant Buddha in Leshan
www.sacred-destinations.com/
china/leshan-giant-buddha.htm
T. +86 (0)833 2302131

**Huanglong Scenic Area
Administration**
www.unep-wcmc.org/sites/wh/
huanglon
T. +86 (0)837 7249000

Kempinski
www.kempinski.com
T. +86 (0) 28 8526 999

JinJiang Hotel
www.jjhotel.com/en
T. +86 (0) 28 8550 6666

Samsara Hotel
www.samsarahotels.com
T. +86 (0) 28 6676 8888

Gingko
7 Fuqin Donglu, Chengdu City,
Sichuan Province
T. +86 (0)28 8777 7788
Open: Dinner Only

Wenshu Temple
Just off Renmin Zhong Lu on
Wenshu Yuan Jie
T. +86 (0)28 674 2375
Open: Lunch

Baguo Buyi
Zo Renmin Nan Lu, 4 Duan
Chengdu
T. +86 (0)28 8553 1688
Open: Dinner only

Xi'an

Xi'an Xianyang Airport
Xi'an Xianyang Airport is located
45 km from the centre of Xi'an
T. +86 (0)29 8879 8486
T. +86 (0)29 8879 8479
T. +86 (0)29 8879 6321
T. +86 (0)29 8879 6260

Terracotta Warriors
Army of Terracotta Warriors
(Bingmayong)
www.bmy.com.cn
T. +86 (0)29 8391 1961 (info)
Open: 8.30 am – 5.30 pm

Gold Buddha in Hua Hin

THAILAND

Chiang Mai | Bangkok | Koh Samui | Hua Hin

THAILAND

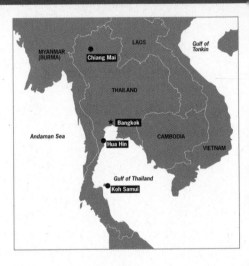

🏆 **Why is this place so special?**

The Kingdom of Thailand draws millions of visitors each year - more than any other country in South East Asia - because of its irresistible combination of breathtaking natural beauty, inspiring temples, welcoming hospitality and healthy cuisine. Thailand also has a rich and colourful culture, many exotic monuments, interesting wildlife and stunning beaches. There is something for everyone, including budget-conscious backpackers, retired couples and those seeking luxurious pampering in a spa.

Thailand offers excellent value for money; there is a variety of reasonably-priced luxury accommodation - so you don't have to slum it in youth hostels - as well as outstanding hostpitality. It's also a great gateway into the rest of South East Asia.

Travellers should find that a couple of weeks are long enough to explore the main sites, although many people can't resist staying for longer.

Many travellers find their experience in Thailand to be a spiritual one. Buddhism is a way of life - not just as a religion, but also as a lifestyle. The numerous temples which are scattered around the country play a central part in daily life. You can observe orange-robed monks leaving the sanctuary of their wats (temples) to receive alms from people on the street. This spiritual influence results in a blend of old tradition with new contemporary living which is magical!

Bangkok must not be missed. It is a dynamic city which is larger than life. The architecture is varied; futuristic high-rise buildings contrast against the glittering Grand Palace. Within Bangkok, travellers will find simple canal and riverside communities, as well as giant outdoor markets which radiate wonderful sounds and scents.

There is a wealth of variety beyond urban Thailand, such as flat plains which feature carpets of rice paddies, dots of tiny villages, high mountains of luxuriant teak forests and the simple beauty of the translucent sea lapping onto endless white, soft sand. Rural life is unhurried and hospitable and behind every Thai smile there is a sense of kindness and wisdom.

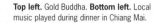
Top left. Gold Buddha. **Bottom left.** Local music played during dinner in Chiang Mai.

You can find all kinds of adventures in Thailand, including extreme sports on land or sea, chance meetings with fellow travellers (and monks!), as well as plenty of spirituality and luxury spas. Gorgeous tropical islands play host to laid-back bungalow guesthouses and five star Thai-style resorts.

Thailand offers something special for every type of traveller. You can choose from national parks in Doi Inthanon, beaches on the coast of the Gulf of Thailand, pulse-pounding dance clubs in Bangkok, or tranquil villages along the Mekong River.

Thai food is famous throughout the Western world, but there is nowhere that it tastes better than in its home country. The cuisine is aromatic and encompasses a unique blend of sweet, sour and salty flavours, which are tempered with fiery spices.

 Fast Facts

Capital: Bangkok

Location: Thailand shares borders with Malaysia, Myanmar (Burma), Laos and Cambodia. The Gulf of Thailand, to the east, and the Andaman Sea, to the west, make up the country's coastlines.

Population: 65,000,000.

Religion: 95% Buddhist, 4% Muslim.

Language: Thai is the official language of Thailand. It is a complicated language with its own alphabet. The main complication is that it is tonal: the same word can could be pronounced with a rising, falling, high, low or level tone and can therefore have five different meanings.

✈ Getting there and exploring around

Getting to Thailand is easy, as Bangkok is one of the main gateways for the Far East, and a stopover point for the rest of Asia and Australasia. The national airline is Thai Airways, which runs direct flights from the UK to Bangkok International Airport. There are other airlines which offer direct routes, such as Eva Air and Qantas Airlines, although they generally stop off for re-fuelling somewhere along the way. Emirates Airlines also operate a route from Manchester or London Heathrow to Bangkok, with a stopover in Dubai.

You can also reach Thailand by boat from its surrounding countries. The main port in Bangkok operates passenger crossings between Thailand and Laos at several points along the Mekong River, but tickets are usually very limited.

Railway to Thailand is also an option. Trains run between Butterworth in Malaysia, and the borders with Cambodia (at Aranyaprathet) and Laos (at Nong Khai). The opulent Eastern and Oriental Express also runs directly from Bangkok to Singapor. If you want to splash out, it's an incredible trip.

Once you've arrived in Thailand, there are a number of options available for transportation within the country. Air travel is a viable option for those on a tight timeframe. Thai Airways International runs services to many major towns, using a total of 12 airports including Phuket and Chiang Mai. Bangkok Airways flies several additional routes including Koh Samui. Discounts are available in off-peak seasons and during special promotional periods. PB Air and Nok Air also fly domestically.

Getting around by water is also possible. Taxi boat ferry services operate along the Chao Phraya River in Bangkok, between Rajburana and Nonthaburi. The services are operated by the Chao Phraya Express Boat company. Ferry services also operate between the mainland and several islands, including Surat Thani to Koh Samui, and Phuket to Phi Phi. Tickets can be booked in person at the dock.

Travelling by rail can be a pleasure in Thailand. State Railways of Thailand runs the excellent railway network linking all major towns, with the exception of Phuket. There are several daily services on each route, with air-conditioned sleeping and restaurant cars on the principal trains. The Southern Line Express stops at Surat Thani for those who wish to continue by bus and ferry to the islands off the east coast.

For those who wish to hire a care, major roads are paved, so driving around Thailand is fairly safe and convenient. Hiring a car is easy, although the minimum age is 21. Alternatively, privately owned air-conditioned buses are comfortable and moderately priced.

☀ Best time of year to visit

Overall, the best time to visit Thailand is between November and February, as it is warm and dry during these months. However, monsoons arrive around July and last into November. This time of year is known as the rainy season and can be uncomfortable.

The peak months tend to be August, November, December, February and March, with secondary peak months in January and July. If your main objective is to avoid the crowds and to take advantage of discounted rooms rates, you should consider travelling during the least crowded months (April, May, June, September and October). On the other hand, it's not difficult to leave the crowds behind, even during peak months, by simply avoiding some of the most popular tourist destinations - such as Phuket.

From top. Floating Market, Koh Samui Sunset, Yoga Retreat.

❓ Must know before you go

Learn the Wai. Present-day Thai society has been shaped by centuries of cultural interchange, particularly with China and India, but more recently with the West. Western visitors will generally receive a handshake on meeting someone. However, a Thai will be greeted with the traditional closed hands and a slight bow of the head - also known as the wai. Visitors should respect this custom and try to adopt the approach. It is also very bad manners to make public displays of anger, as Thais regard such behavior as boorish and a loss of 'face'.

Bangkok Beware. In Bangkok, unlicensed taxis, recognisable by their black and white license plates, should be avoided. This is most relevant for solo women travelling at night. Look for licensed taxis that have yellow and black license plates. Also be aware that the number of drink-spiking incidents in Bangkok is on the rise.

Make merit. While many Thai people will 'make merit' on a daily basis, it's possible for visitors to participate in this age-old tradition as well. This custom, aims to secure a better life here and hereafter, can be performed in any number of ways: offer daily objects like soap, foods, robes, or a small donation to the Abbott of a monastery; contribute to a monk's morning meal with offerings of food; or purchase a caged bird at one of the temple complexes and set it free. It is best to talk to a Thai person about formalities and customs beforehand, in order to understand the etiquette. And remember, always thank the receiving monk, he will never thank you. He never begs he only offers you the opportunity to better your life.

🖼 Highlights

Markets in Bangkok and Chiang Mai. Market shopping can be a full-contact sport and there are a variety of venues where you can pick up fine local crafts and jewellery. The busy markets are certainly the most atmospheric. Choose from Chatuchak, the weekend market in Bangkok, or the busy night bazaar in Chiang Mai and the many small markets in every small town.

Diving in the Gulf of Thailand. Incredible diving and gorgeous beaches await the intrepid traveller. Head to Koh Samui or Koh Tao.

Yoga and Spa Retreats. Take time out and experience some of the best spa treatments, relaxation breaks and yoga retreats in the world. You will return a different person.

Temple Charm. Buddhism is the centre of all Thai culture. It's impossible to miss some of the incredible temples scattered around the country. Head to Wat Phra Kaeo in Bangkok or Wat Phra Singh in Chiang Mai.

Adventure: City Slicker
Destination: Bangkok

✛ Regional Information

Also referred to as Thailand's 'City of Angels', Bangkok is a place where possibilities are limited only by the imagination. You'll marvel at the glories of the past and delight in the golden opportunities of the present. It is modern and westernised, but every so often you get a glimpse of a temple, which reminds you of Bangkok's spiritual past.

The influence of the city's past is not limited to major temples. Files of orange-robed Buddhist monks making their early morning rounds, for example, present a scene which has essentially remained unaltered by the passing of time. Today's backdrop of high-rise buildings only adds wonder to Bangkok's traditional sights, from which the city continues to draw its identity.

Ultimately, Bangkok derives its unique 'flavour' from its people. They are fun-loving and easy going and seem to possess a tolerance and patience which permeates throughout the city to give a real feeling of freedom. At times, Bangkok may appear to be hectic and disorganised, but its final essence is a good-natured acceptance of life with all its eccentricities.

The list of attractions include: The Grand Palace, classical Thai dances, floating markets, crazy nightclubs, world class museums and awe inspiring temples - not to mention exquisite spicy Thai cuisine. Three or four days should be enough for you to experience the highlights.

The Grand Palace and Wat Pra Kaeo form the city's most important landmarks, perched on a huge compound surrounded by a white wall. The Grand Palace has an area of about 1.5 square km and includes the Royal Chapel, the Royal Collection of Weapons, the Coin Pavillion, and a small museum containing artifacts from the palace. The grandest of the buildings is the Chakri Maha Prasad, an impressive three-spired building which represents a mixture of Thai and Western architecture and is not to be missed.

Adventure: City Slicker
Destination: Bangkok

One of the most visited attractions in Bangkok is Jim Thompson's House, a beautifully preserved traditional Thai house. Jim Thompson, an American and former member of the US Office of Strategic Services (OSS), came to Thailand during World War II. After the war he revived the flagging silk weaving industry but disappeared under mysterious circumstances in 1967 in the Cameron Highlands in Malaysia. The house contains fine antiques and artworks from all over South East Asia and is definitely worth a visit.

The Thailand National Museum is the largest museum in South East Asia and is an excellent place to learn about Thai art. All periods and styles are represented, from Dvaravati to Ratanakosin, and there's also a well-maintained collection of traditional musical instruments from Thailand, Laos, Cambodia and Indonesia. Other permanent exhibits include ceramics, clothing and textiles, woodcarving, royal regalia, as well as Chinese art and weaponry. The museum's grounds contain the restored Buddhaisawan (Phutthaisawan) Chapel. Inside the chapel (built in 1795) are some well-preserved original murals and one of the country's most revered Buddha images, Phra Phuttha Sihing. Legend has it that the image came from Ceylon, but art historians attribute it to the 13th century Sukhothai period. Be aware though, the museum isn't air-conditioned and English signage is irregular. However, tours are available in foreign languages.

Wat Arun, the golden Temple of Dawn, shimmers in the sun besides the Chao Phraya River. As you climb its steep central prang (tower), you get a close-up view of the porcelain pieces that make up its floral design. Before evening falls, take a boat along Damnoen Saduak, Bangkok's most popular floating market, where you can buy some amazing types of fruit, such as the famous Malacca grape, Chinese grapefruit, mangoes, bananas and coconut. The excellent quality soil beside the 32 km canal is very fertile for growing many kinds of fruit and vegetables. There you can also see traditional Thai houses, and the way they travel on the water. Although the floating market is 105 km from Bangkok, this is usually a worthwhile trip.

Bangkok's nightlife has a reputation for being wild and eccentric. But at the same time, it's fairly safe and lots of fun. Once only known for its 'lady boy shows', it has rapidly developed into the coolest capital city in Asia. You can enjoy great jazz bars, trendy clubs and chic restaurants which always offer service with a smile, of course!

Khao Sarn Road, which was a featured scene in the film and novel The Beach, has long been a haunt for budget backpackers. Along this road there are guesthouses, budget hotels, restaurants and pubs with friendly atmospheres. There are also lots of shops and food stalls which make for a lively night out and a good place to meet fellow travellers.

Siam Niramit is one of Thailand's must-see shows. 'A Journey to the Enchanted Kingdom of Siam' features an enormous stage with over 150 performers, 500 lavish costumes, spectacular scenery, and amazing special effects. In addition to the show, you can stroll through a simulated traditional Thai village located in the grounds and soak up the atmosphere of Thai life.

Stylish Places to Stay

Zen Style: Davis Bangkok. This hotel has cleverly mixed the extremes of modern and traditional styles. It offers a place of strange but luxurious contradiction. Offering everything from spa suites to luxury Thai villas, with decorative themes of 'Versace' and 'Florida', the Davis has taken the concept of boutique to a whole new level. The Feng Shui swimming pool is a classic.

Royal Style: Sukothai. Modelled on the ancient capital of Sukhothai, this exquisite tribute to Thai architectural heritage is a stunning sanctuary. Serene buddhas overlook inner ponds, ambient music meanders down hushed hallways, while artifacts and orchids pose calmly in hidden corners. The suites offer a soothing décor of gun-metal silk tones, burnt orange and ochre, hardwood floors and stone carvings. Bathrooms have porcelain tubs and are filled with fabulous bath products. It's not just the fluffy robes that make you feel like royalty. ☆

Hip Style: Metropolitan. If you expect attention to detail from a hotel, you won't be disappointed at the Metropolitan. From Armani-clad bellmen to commissioned beauty products, from morning yoga to original artworks, and from Bose sound equipment to organic gastronomy, you'll be 100% satisfied. The Met is popular with jet-setting couples, celebrities, Hollywood directors and hip business folk. A-list stars love the immense penthouse with its two-storey windows, private lift and 24-hour butler.

Delicious Places to Eat

Veggie Thai: May Kaidee. This restaurant appears to consist of simple tables in an alleyway, but looks can be deceiving. Vegetarians can choose from a limited picture menu, or they can write down their own order. The service can be hit or miss, but it's always friendly. May Kaidee offers some of the best authentic Thai food going and it's all vegetarian.

Bed hopping: Bed Supper Club. Ever wanted to get into bed with Bangkok's young, hip elite? That's what it's all about at ultra-modern Bed Supper Club. Diners are feted from a limited menu nightly and you can sit (or lay) on huge beds, noshing and hobnobbing to the tunes of a house DJ. Great food and a unique atmosphere. ☆

Thai Treats: Ton Pho. Catch a breeze at this open-air riverside restaurant. Ceiling fans rotate relentlessly as waiters scurry across the wooden floorboards. Also, be careful if you're wearing high heels - there are big gaps between the floorboards which reveal the river beneath.

Adventure: Culture Vulture
Destination: Chiang Mai

✈ **Regional Information**

Chiang Mai, Thailand's second largest city, has a striking backdrop of Doi Suthep (one of Thailand's holiest temples). The city is home to over 300 temples, several national parks and a quaint historical aura. It is also a modern, friendly and international city with a lot to discover for the culture vulture traveller. The city is buzzing with excitement during the day and the night. A stay of five days should be sufficient to get the most out of this area, although a longer stay would enable you to visit the Golden Triangle - where the borders of Thailand, Burma and Laos meet.

The best time to visit Chiang Mai is between October and April. The rest of the year can be a virtual monsoon washout. Cultural festivals occur throughout the year, with the bulk of them between late December and April. These provide a great opportunity to immerse yourself in traditional Thai culture. Chiang Mai is a particularly fun and refreshing spot to experience the wetness of the Songkhran 'water splashing' festival.

Situated in the old town, Wat Chiang Man is the oldest temple in the city. Founded by King Mengrai in 1296, it features typical Northern Thai temple architecture with massive teak columns inside the *bòt* (central sanctuary). There are two important Buddha images in a cabinet to the right. The first image, Phra Sila, stands about 25 cm tall, and reputedly came from Sri Lanka or India around 2,500 years ago. Chances are that it isn't quite that old (Buddha images weren't created for about another 500 years), but it's still an extremely impressive and revered artifact. The other, a crystal seated Buddha only 10 cm in height, is about 1,800 years old. Known as the Phra Satang Man, it was shunted back and forth between Thailand and Laos for centuries before finding a permanent home at Chiang Mai.

Chiang Mai's most visited Buddhist temple, Wat Phra Singh, owes its fame to the fact that it houses the holy Phra Singh (Lion Buddha). Architecturally the temple is a perfect example of the classic Northern Thai (or Lanna) style which can be followed from Chiang Mai to Luang Prabang.

The Phra Singh Buddha supposedly comes from Sri Lanka, although it is not particularly Singhalese in style. It is identical to two images in Nakhon Si Thammarat and Bangkok and, as is typical for a famous Buddha image, it has quite a travel history (Sukhothai, Ayuthaya, Chiang Rai, Luang Prabang). As such, no one really knows whether it is the original Phra Singh Buddha, nor can anyone document its place of origin, but it is an interesting specimen all the same.

For a scenic treat, you should head to Thailand's highest point, the Doi Inthanon National Park, which is aptly named 'the roof of Thailand'. The summit of Doi Inthanon, at 2,596 meters, has a climate which is more like Canada than Thailand. Given that the main attractions are spread over a distance of 40 km, we recommend you travel there using private transportation as this will allow flexibility in planning your itinerary.

Mae Klang Waterfall and its surrounding area is a fantastic location. This unusual waterfall has been visited by Thai people for many years. On sunny days, they arrive in large numbers to swim, picnic and relax in this beautiful setting. The waterfall and its rapids spill over a wide exposure of granite rock and you can get up pretty close. Rappelling down the waterfall is an option for the brave. You can also rock climb, or hike in the area. A Chiang Mai-based adventure company, The Peak Adventure, can arrange trips and transport to the waterfall for you. The company is located near the night bazaar (see Highlights on page 139).

Adventure: Culture Vulture
Destination: Chiang Mai

Thailand's gentle elephants never fail to amaze visitors to Thailand. It isn't uncommon to see elephants padding along city streets. These huge creatures can be daunting at first. But once you spend some time around them you will be reassured that they are intelligent, graceful and majestic. There are many elephant camps in and around Chiang Mai. These camps offer a good entrée into the world of elephants. Tourists can also get close to these creatures by taking elephant rides, especially in resort areas. Animal cruelty activists claim that this practice involves an element of cruelty to the elephants, as the handlers can sometimes abuse the elephants and keep them in substandard conditions. Officials claim that this practice is coming to an end, but elephants are still used in big cities as ploys to make moeny from diners and shoppers. It is a pity to see these majestic creatures wandering in traffic with blinking lights hanging from their tails, and it is tempting to buy some sugar cane to feed to them. However, we recommend that you refrain from temptation and give you money to a more worthwhile charity. By donating money to these 'street traders', you are encouraging the handlers to continue with their business.

By far the best way to get to know an elephant is to visit elephants at the Young Elephant Training Centre in Lampang, 150 km south of Chiang Mai. Visitors can sign up for a trek at the centre, although it is something you can just dip in and out of. You'll be given a set of baggy elephant trainer togs and will be taught the language of the elephants. You'll spend the better part of a day caring for the animals, feeding and washing them as well as learning all that you need to know to be able to hop on the neck and steer your own elephant. On multi-day treks you'll be assigned your own animal and will ride alone. It's a great experience for those who like to really get involved with the local wildlife.

As daytime falls, Chiang Mai comes alive. The night market sprawls into the streets with local vendors selling everything from jewellery to incense. The origins of the market date back to the days when the Yunnanese trading caravans used to stop near the Ping River along an ancient trade route. Good things to buy here include denim, Northern and North Eastern hand-woven fabrics, yâam (shoulder bags), hill-tribe crafts (many tribes people set up their own stalls here and the Akha tribe wander around on foot!), opium scales, hats, silver jewellery, lacquerware, woodcarvings, and iron and bronze Buddhas. Don't forget to barter!

Stylish Places to Stay

Minimal Style: The Chedi. The Chedi is the epitome of luxury and style. It offers local décor and minimalist post-colonial architecture. All rooms have private terraces, huge bathtubs and river views. The weary traveller could spend days in its lush spa and the incredibly equipped fitness center, which also offers yoga classes. The old Manila-style consulate building near the river is dedicated to the restaurant which serves northern Thai and Pacific Rim cuisine. You won't want to move. ☆

Chic Boutique Style: D2. Billing itself as a 'lifestyle hotel', the 130 room D2 has renovated a building which was formerly occupied by the Chiang Inn and transformed it into a comfortable, eye-pleasing fusion of modern European minimalism with Thai colours and textures. Although it is not as plush as the Chedi, is has a great location in the centre of the night market. D2 is trendy and attracts a young hip crowd. It has an outdoor pool and Devarana spa. Overall, it's good value for money.

Monastery Style: Rachamankha. Owned by a well-known local interior designer and currently the rage among visiting glitterati. Tucked away down a narrow street behind Wat Phra Sing, it consists of a quadrangle of rooms fronted by full length porticoes, reminiscent of a Buddhist monastery cloister in 16th century Northern Thailand. Another two storey wing surrounding an ample swimming pool contains a library for the exclusive use of hotel guests. Artifacts and authentic art pieces are everywhere.

Delicious Places to Eat

Outdoor dining: Galare Food Centre. This is a big indoor and outdoor cluster of permanent vendors located opposite the main Chiang Mai night bazaar building. There are a variety of dining options and Thai classical dancing occurs nightly.

Northern Thai delights: Heuan Phen. This is a classy establishment which is highly regarded for northern Thai food. Among the house specialties are Chiang Mai and Jiin Haw (Chinese Muslim) dishes, such as lâap khûa (northern-style minced-meat salad), náam phrík nùm (chilli sauce made with roasted eggplant) and aahãan phéun meuang (local food).

Authentic Thai: Khrua Phuket Laikhram. This small family-run restaurant near Chiang Mai University is worth hunting down for its delicious, cheap and authentic home style Southern Thai cooking. It also has an upstairs dining room to cater for groups. There are no English menus so you may have to improvise with your phrasebook.

Adventure: Beach Bum
Destination: Koh Samui

✈ Regional Information

Koh Samui, or Samui Island (in Thai 'Koh' means 'Island') has long been the destination for paradise-seeking travellers of all types. Its turquoise waters and sandy bays are lined with thatched roofed bungalows and resorts, a plethora of restaurants to satisfy hungry connoisseurs, and the thumping nightlife of beach parties. This is the place that coined the term 'beach bum'. Whether you want a busy bustling beach or quiet secluded sands, there are many options for you to spend your lazy days. For those wanting gentle adventures, there are interesting rock formations, national parks, markets and Thai cooking classes. If you are visiting during December or January then the scuba diving can be superb. A week is usually enough time to relax here, but you may want longer if you have been travelling long haul and need a break.

Getting to Koh Samui is easy. Flights from Bangkok are regular and only take an hour. Those wanting a bit more adventure can take the intrepid backpacker route and jump on the train from Hua Lumphong Railway Station down to Surat Thani. From Surat Thani you will have to go to the harbour to catch a ferry for a pleasant two-hour ride to the island. First class sleepers are the best option for the train journey from Bangkok to Surat Thani.

You can take a day trip from Koh Samui to the Ang Thong national marine park, an archipelago of about 40 islands comprising this idyllic destination. A couple of tour operators run day trips to the park. It became popular when Alex Garland's novel 'The beach' hit the silver screens featuring Leonardo DiCaprio as an intrepid traveller in search of a utopian beach society. Limestone cliffs, hidden lagoons, white sandy beaches and dense vegetation provide postcard-perfect scenery everywhere you look. The numerous caves and crevices are home to nesting swallows, and there's a narrow coral reef in the south west of the park.

Adventure: Beach Bum
Destination: Koh Samui

There are plenty of accessible beaches on Koh Samui so you don't need to worry if your guesthouse is not on the beach. If you are staying at an upmarket resort, it is more than likely that your hotel will have some of its own private beach. Chaweng Beach is perfect if you like the beach, but don't want to feel like you're marooned. The beach covers a large part of Kao Sumai's north eastern coast and offers countless options for dining, shopping, nightlife and water sports. Chaweng can be a lot of fun and parties last late into the night with raucous little clubs and young crowds.

If you prefer a beach with a more intimate atmosphere, head to Mae Nam Beach. Quiet and calm, with just a few comfortable hotels and small bungalow resorts, Mae Nam is much less crowded than Chaweng Beach. The water is clean and deep and is excellent for swimming. Visitors tend to be more mature and relaxed.

Bo Phut Beach is a backpacker's paradise. The peaceful bay lies between Mae Nam Beach and Phra Yai Beach on Koh Samui's Northern coast. It is good for swimming in parts, but it also offers port facilities and a stretch of seafood restaurants.

If seafood is your forte, then head to the restaurants in Bo Phut Beach - known to be one of the best areas on Koh Samui for seafood. You can also find a number of economically priced bungalows there.

Lamai Beach is mainly visited for the rocky Hin Ta and Hin Yai ('grandfather' and 'grandmother'), two phallic-like symbols carved by the forces of nature, which have to be seen to be believed. It is easy to swim here and the waters are clear enough to snorkel.

Cheung Mon Beach is peaceful and tranquil and is situated in the north east of Koh Samui, south of Thon Sai Bay and closer to Samui airport. The beach has white sands and is exceptionally beautiful.

Tongsai Bay is a private beach with a world-renowned resort. Although small, this beach has gained popularity due to its proximity to first-class accommodation.

If you want a break from the beach, visiting Na Muang Falls makes a nice afternoon trip. Na Muang Falls is 30 metres high and is the tallest waterfall on Samui. The water cascades over amazing purple rocks and there's a great pool for swimming at the base. This is the most scenic of Samui's falls, and is also one of the least popular among visitors.

One of Koh Samui's most famous attractions is its nightlife, and in particular, the full moon parties. The parties are normally hosted on Haad Rin beach on the nearby island of Ko Phangan and they attract about 10,000 to 20,000 people every month. Paint yourself in UV colours and let your body lose control. There are also many small tables on the beach where you can sit down and meet fellow travellers from all parts of the globe. You can order drinks and food from the restaurants and the bars next to the Had Rin Nok beach. But beware - use only licensed boats. For those wanting a more relaxing evening, prepare yourself for some steamy cooking classes. The Samui Institute of Thai Culinary Arts offers daily Thai-cooking classes, as well as courses in the aristocratic Thai art of carving fruit and vegetables into intricate floral designs.

Romance Style: Tongsai Bay and Cottages.
Unwind in the beautiful surroundings of Tongsai Bay, with a private beach, tubs on the terrace and a gorgeous little tea room. The spa is world class and offers wonderful Thai massages, which stretch and bend you to release tension and stress. ⭐

Design Style: The Library. This elegant minimalist structure is set in a lush environment on Chaweng Beach. It is divided into 26 suites, or studio cabins, so the complex avoids the ugly hotel complex look. The cabins have been discreetly scattering into lush vegetation. Every studio has its own personal computer with broadband connection and plasma television. Suites include jacuzzis while studios sport bathtubs with rain showers. ⭐

Thai Style: Muang Kulaypan. This hotel is located at the far north end of Chaweng beach away from all the parties and madness. The architect used simple raw materials for the construction and many local craftworks for decoratation. The rooms are slick with black tiled bathrooms and a siphon-shaped sink, accompanied with lemongrass soaps. They also offer free transport from the airport.

🍴 Delicious Places to Eat

Eclectic International: Rocky's Restaurant.
Rocky's pride themselves on fine quality cuisine and seem to spend hours in the kitchen preparing delightful dishes of international flavour. Located in Lamai Beach.

Thai-fusion treats: The Five Islands Restaurant.
The open air architecture and design of Balinese and Thai origin create an exotic ambiance of tropical paradise at this eatery. They serve fresh and exotic Thai food in a romantic setting on the beach.

Fish Fun: Starfish & Coffee. This is one of the longest established restaurants in Fisherman's Village and is also one of its most atmospheric. It is split into separate dining and bar areas and plays ambient music which creates a 'Buddha-Bar-On-Sea' vibe.

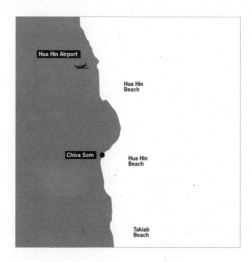

Hua Hin Airport

Hua Hin Beach

Chiva Som

Hua Hin Beach

Takiab Beach

Focus On...
Yoga retreat in Hua Hin

Yoga and spa lovers should brace themselves for the most indulgent retreat in the world - Chiva Som. Guaranteed to help you lose weight, tone up, detox, stop smoking or generally improve your health - this place is pure heaven.

Chiva Som is a new beginning for many. One of the finest high-end health resorts in the region, this ultra-peaceful campus is a collection of handsome pavilions, bungalows and central buildings dressed in fine teak and sea-colored tiles, nestled in landscaped grounds just beyond a pristine beach.

But what brings so many to Chiva Som is its spa programmes. From Chi Gong to chin-ups, and from muscle straining to massage, a stay at Chiva Som is a chance to escape the world of hard work and focus on the development of your body and your mind. Leave the kids at home, turn off the mobiles and change your dress to loose-fitting cotton.

Upon check-in, you'll fill out an extensive survey, have a brief medical check and meet with a counsellor who can tailor a program to fit your needs, goals and budget.

You can focus on early-morning yoga, stretching and tough workouts, or go for gentle massages, aromatherapy, even isolation chambers and past-life regression workshops.

The choices are many and personal trainers, staff and facilities are unmatched in the region. The resort's spa cuisine is not all granola and oats, but a simple and healthy affair, and there is a nice bond that develops between guests and staff in weekly barbecues and frequent 'mocktail' parties. You will also meet other like-minded travellers from all walks of life. The spa treatments are fantastic: don't pass up their signature Chiva Som Massage.

After experiencing Chiva Som's beauty and health treatments, you'll know exactly how the rich and famous are able to stay so healthy. A visit here can be a good place to start a new 'chapter' of health.

Opposite page. Gold Buddha in Hua Hin

ⓘ Stylish Essentials

General Information

Bangkok Tourist Bureau
17/1 Phra Athit
T. +66 (0) 2225 7612 (info)
Hours: 9.00am-7.00pm

Tourist Authority of Thailand
1600 New Phetburi Road 10310
The Tourist Authority of Thailand
(TAT) has offices throughout the
country and are helpful for bus
schedules, local maps, and finding
accommodation.
www.tat.or.th

Traveler information and tours
www.discoverthailand.com

Thai Airways
www.thaiairways.com
T. 020 7491-7953 (UK Sales &
Reservations)

Eva Air
www.evaair.com
T. 020 7380-8300 (UK Sales &
Reservations)

Emirates Airlines
www.emirates.com

Qantas Airlines
www.qantas.com

Bangkok Air
www.bangkokair.com

PB Air
www.pbair.com

Nok Air
www.nokair.co.th

Main port of Bangkok
www.bkp.port.co.th

Getting There and Around by Rail

State Of Thailand Railways
www.thailandrailway.com
T. +66 (02) 222 0175

Eastern and Oriental Express
www.orient-express.com
T. 0845 077 2222, within the UK

Chao Phraya Express Boat
www.chaophrayaboat.co.th
T. +66 (02) 623 6143

Airports

**Bangkok International (BKK)
(Suvarnabhumi)**
www.airportthai.co.th
To/from the airport: There are airport
express bus routes to the city. There
are also regular public bus routes to
the city and to the provinces,
including Pattaya. An overhead city
rail link is being built and is expected
to open by December 2007. Taxis are
also available at all hours.
Facilities: Left luggage, first aid,
chemist, duty-free shop, banks,
bureaux de change, restaurants, bars
and snack bars, post office,
international and local car hire,
accommodation reservations,
and Internet cafe.

**Chiang Mai International Airport
(CNX)**
www.airportthai.co.th
To/from the airport: Taxi services are
available to the city centre.
Facilities: International and local car
hire companies, banks/bureaux de
change, restaurant, shops and bar.

Phuket International Airport (HKT)
www.airportthai.co.th
To/from the airport: Taxis and
limousines are available to the
city center.
Facilities: Left luggage, duty-free
shops, first aid, bureau de change,
post office, restaurant and snack
bars, international and local car hire
companies and tourist information.

Bangkok

General Information
www.bangkok.com

Grand Palace and Wat Pra Kaeo
Located between two old temple;
Wat Phra Chetuphon (Wat Pho) to the
south and Wat Mahathat (Wat Salak)
to the north.
Open: Daily from 8.30 am - 3.30 pm.
Price: Admission is 125 baht.

National Museum
Th Na Phra That
T. +66 (0) 2224 1333 (info)

Jim Thompson House
www.jimthompson.com
www.jimthompsonhouse.com

Siam Niramit
19 Tiamruammit Road, Huaykwang,
opposite the Thailand Cultural Centre,
Bangkok 10320
www.siamniramit.com
T. +66 (0) 2649-9222
E. reservation@siamniramit.com
F. +66 (0) 2649-9275

Damnoen Saduak Floating Market
Travel from Bangkok via
Thonburi-Paktoh Highway to
Samut Songkhram Town.
Follow the sign to Damnoen
Saduak (Highway No.325).

Erawan Shrine
The Erawan Shrine is centrally located
next to the Erawan Hotel on Rajadamri
Road, diagonally opposite the World
Trade Centre. There is no entrance
fee, but you will be encouraged to
purchase flowers and incense, etc.
from the vendors around the shrine
and you should make a donation if
you can.

Khao Sarn Road
www.khaosanroad.com

Davis Bangkok
www.davisbangkok.net
T. +66 2 260-8000

Sukhothai
www.sukhothai.com
T. +66 (0) 2 344 8888

Metropolitan
www.metropolitan.como.bz/bangkok/
T. +66 (0) 2 625 3333

May Kaidee
T. +66 (0) 2629 4839

Bed Supper Club
26 Soi Sukhumvit 11,Sukhumvit
Road, Klongtoey-nua, Wattana,
Bangkok 10110
www.bedsupperclub.com
T. +66 (0) 2651-3537
Open: 7.30 – 9.30

Ton Pho
Th Phra Athit
T. +66 (0) 2280 0452
Open: 10.00 am – 10.00 pm

Koh Samui

General info
www.kohsamui.org

Ang Thong National Marine Park
T. +66 (0) 7728 0222 (info)

**Tour Company to Ang Thong
National Marine Park**
www.tourskohsamui.com/angthong.
html

Planet Scuba Diving Company
www.planet-scuba.net
T.+66 (0) 77 422 386
E. Info@planet-scuba.net

**The Samui Institute of Thai
Culinary Arts**
46/6 Soi Colibri
www.sitca.net
T. +66 (0) 7741 3434 (info)

Tongsai Bay & Cottages
www.tongsaibay.co.th
T. +66 (0) 77 245 480

The Library
www.thelibrary.name
T. +66 (0) 77 422 7678

Muang Kulaypan Hotel
www.kulaypan.com
T. +66 (0) 77 230 850

Rocky's Restaurant
www.rockyresort.com
T. +66 (0) 77 233 020
Open: Dinner

Five Islands Restaurant
www.thefiveislands.com
T. +66 (0) 7745 5359
Open: Dinner

Starfish & Coffee
Fisherman's Village, 51/7, Moo 1,
Tambon Bo Phut
T. +66 (0) 7742 7201
Open: all day dining

Chiang Mai

TAT Office
TAT Northern Office
105/1 Chiangmai-Lamphun Road,
Amphur Muang, Chinagmai
T. +66 (0) 53 248 604
E. tatcnx@samart.co.th

General Information
www.chiangmai-thai.com

Wat Chiang Man
off Th Ratchaphakhinai
Open: 9.00 am – 5.00 pm

Wat Phra Singh
Th Singarat
T. +66 (0) 5381 4164 (info)

Doi Inthanom Rapelling
The Peak Adventure Company
302/4 Chiangmai Lumphum Rd, T.
Watgate A.Muang Chiangmai
www.thepeakadventure.com
T.+66 (0) 53 - 800567
E. info@thepeakadventure.com

Doi Inthanon National Park
119 Ban-Luang Chomtong Chiangmai
50160
Amphur Chom Thong Chiang Mai
T. +66 (0) 5326 8550
E. inthanon_np@hotmail.com

**Young Elephant Training Centre
in Lampang**
T. +66 (0) 54 22 9042

Maetamann Elephant Camp
535 Rimtai, Maerim, Chiang Mai
50180
T. +66 (0) 5329 7060

Become an Elephant Mahout
Lampang, near Chiang Mai
T. +66 (0) 5422 9042

D2 Hotel
www.d2hotels.com
T. +66 (0) 5399 9999

The Chedi
www.ghmhotels.com
T. +66 (0) 53 253 333

Rachamankha
www.rachamankha.com
T. +66 (0) 53 90 4111

Galare Food Centre
Th Chang Khlan, opposite the Night
Bazaar Building, has a large open-air
food court, featuring free Thai
classical dance performances nightly.
All food is paid for with coupons;
most mains 20-50 baht.

Heuan Phen
112 Th Rachamankha
T.+66 (0) 5327 7103 (info)
Open: 8.30 am – 3.30 pm
& 5.00 pm – 10.00 pm

Khrua Phuket Laikhram
1/10 Th Suthep
T. +66 (0) 5327 8909 (info)
Open: 8.00 am – 2.00 pm
& 4.00 pm – 8.30 pm

Hua Hin

**Chiva Som Chiva-Som
International Health Resort**
Chiva-Som, 73/4 Petchkasem Road,
Hua Hin, Thailand 77110
www.chivasom.com
T. +66 (0) 3253-6536
F. +66 (0) 32 511 154
E. reserv@chivasom.com
Price: 5-day Single package from
£2,000 per person

Pizzeria Da Baffetto, Rome.

ITALY

Rome | Amalfi Coast | Florence | Cinque Terre

🏆 Why is this place so special?

Italy is stylish, cultured, good humoured and full of energy. For centuries, painters and poets have been inspired by its golden light, its stunning landscapes and its rich cultural heritage. The country's sumptuous landscapes seem to have been made for romance, while its culture and its cuisine seduce just about everyone who goes there. Its history, which spans three millennia, tells the story of a country which has had a strong influence over Europe's development. This influence is particularly apparent in the case of culture, style, architecture, religion, political and economic thought, creativity and artistic design.

Italy's major cities have individual characteristics. Rome is about grandeur, history and haste. Florence, the cradle of the Renaissance, is a masterpiece of studied elegance. Venice is ethereal and mysterious. Milan has powerhouse pace. Naples is fiery with its dramatic backdrop of Mount Vesuvius.

There is a huge variety of things to do throughout Italy. You can visit Roman ruins, study Renaissance art, stay in quaint medieval hill towns, ski in the Alps, explore the canals of Venice, or gaze at beautiful churches. You can also indulge in the pleasures of *la dolce vita* (the sweet life) by eating good food, drinking good wine and improving your wardrobe.

Throughout Italy's countryside, you can visit vineyards and cellars to taste the very best regional wines, workshops where crafts are produced by hand, and friendly *trattoria* (locally owned cafés rather than a formal restaurant) where simple but superb dishes are served. Nobody in the world does pasta and pizzas like the Italians, especially the Neapolitan pizza with a thin crust and lots of topping.

Cooking styles vary notably from region to region. The region of Emilia-Romagna has produced some of Italy's best-known dishes, namely Spaghetti Bolognese, Lasagne and Tortellini. The region of Liguria is the home of pesto, the mainstay of Italian recipes worldwide.

If you want to buy food from a supermarket, you'll find it difficult to spot any national chains - the Italians prefer to shop in small independent stores which sell specialised local delicacies.

Italy's beautiful landscapes, stunning sunsets, fine wine and endearing waiters make it a fabulous destination for romantics. There can be few experiences which are as amorous as wandering the little streets in the heart of Rome, or draining another glass of *limoncello* (a strong lemon liqueur, not for the faint-hearted) on a terrace on the Amalfi Coast.

A wealth of accommodation is available for those who are looking for peace, relaxation and tranquility. Hideaway retreats in the countryside and scenic hilltop *palazzos* (palaces) offer an ideal place for a honeymoon or a romantic break. To experience some of the country's highlights, a week or two is best. But for a short weekend break then we recommend a trip to one the cities. But be warned - once you arrive you will be hooked and back for more.

📖 Fast Facts

Capital: Rome.

Location: Italy is instantly recognisable on a map thanks to its boot shape. It is surrounded by the Adriatic, Ionian, Ligurian and Tyrrhenian Seas - all of which form part of the Mediterranean Sea. The Alps, in the north, separate Italy from France, Switzerland, Austria and Slovenia.

Population: 58,462,375.

Religion: 84% Roman Catholic, 6% other (Protestants, Jews and Muslims).

Language: Standard Italian, but numerous local dialects are spoken.

✈ Getting there and exploring around

Getting to Italy from the UK and the rest of Europe is relatively easy and can be very reasonably priced. There are many low-cost direct flights to Italy. Alitalia is the national airline. It offers direct flights from the UK to both Rome and Milan. British Airways and BMI fly direct routes from London to Naples. Other low-cost airlines include Thomsonfly, RyanAir and Easyjet. Many routes change from season to season, so it is always best to check online.

You can also reach Italy by train from London. There are a variety of routes to choose from. However, if you want to do this journey in style, take the Orient Express train from London - via Paris and Venice - to Rome. It takes four days and allows you to linger over some beautiful scenery.

Once you've arrived in Italy, the most flexible and fun way to get around is by car. Roads are generally good, and there is an excellent network of *autostrada* (freeways), although you do have to pay tolls. Be careful in city centres, especially Rome, as the locals drive quite recklessly.

Other means of transport within Italy include domestic air travel and railway. Domestic air travel can be costly and is probably only worth doing if you are really short of time. However, railway services are generally simple, cheap and efficient. Two of Italy's famous islands, Sicily and Sardinia, can be reached by ferry from the mainland and are definitely worth a visit. You can reach Sicily from Naples, Civitavecchia, Reggio di Calabria, Livorno and Genoa. Sardinia can be reached from Genoa, La Spezia, Civitavecchia, Livorno, Naples, Tràpani and Palermo.

☞ Best time of year to visit

Geographically, Italy has a good mixture of weather conditions. Its mountain regions endure harsher winters, including September snowfalls, while temperatures and conditions begin to moderate as you head South. The North is the wettest area, and the wettest months are between October and December. It can also rain quite heavily on the Amalfi Coast during Spring (April to May).

On the whole, Italy is at its best in Spring and Autumn (October to November). During these seasons the scenery is especially beautiful, the temperatures are pleasant, and there are fewer crowds. That said, if you are visiting Italy during the summer, try to avoid August.

Most Italians take their summer holiday, or 'la ferragosta', in August and, as such, many shops and businesses are closed. On the other hand, the most popular tourist areas can get extremely busy during August. If large crowds of noisy Italians at the beach is not your cup of tea, then steer clear.

Opposite page, Top. Four Rivers Fountain, Rome. **Bottom.** Streets of Sienna.

? Must know before you go

The language of love. Italians like to talk and when they do, they use their hands expressively. Get to grips with the language and learn a few phrases before you go. The effort will be really appreciated, and before you know it, you might be having a full-blown conversation in Italian!

Children are sacred. If you happen to be travelling with children, remember that Italians put children at the heart of the family (and at the head of the table!) Your children will be more than looked after, in fact they will be spoilt rotten!

Obsession with football. Italians are passionate about football, calcio (men), women and grandmothers included! Everywhere you go they will be watching their favourite team or reading the national sport newspaper, Gazetta Dello Sport. If you get a chance, watch a match and enjoy the atmosphere.

Highlights

Shopping in Rome. Rome is a shopping heaven. You can buy everything from famous Italian designer fashion to local art. Head to Via Borgogne, where you will be lured into some of the most famous shops in the world and most probably charmed into buying something you don't need.

Coastline of Amalfi. Giant lemons line the coast in this Southern treat. The winding roads and quaint pretty villages offer some of the best panoramic views in Europe.

Culture of Florence. Striking buildings, formidable galleries and treasure-crammed churches - explore the immense culture that Florence has to offer.

Adventure: City Slicker
Destination: Rome

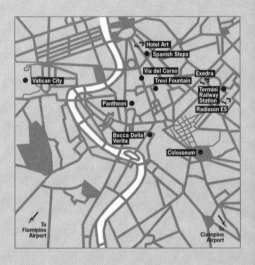

⚜ Regional Information

Rome is littered with relics which are up to 2,000 years old. As such, it exerts an enduring fascination over its many visitors. It's difficult to pinpoint the most popular aspect of 'The Eternal City', as it is sometimes referred. However, a shortlist of the most popular aspects must include the opulence of the Vatican, the gory resonance of the Colosseum, the mystery of the *Bocca Della Verita* (Mouth of Truth) and the city's inspiring café culture. One thing is for sure, however, Rome is seriously addictive.

Monuments of ancient times and splendours of the Baroque period form a wonderful backdrop to the modern-day buzz of well-heeled Italians, swarming scooters and vibrant street cafés. Rome has an overwhelming breadth of designer shops, and style is something that the city's residents take very seriously. Don't get caught out though - remember to dress appropriately. Most Romans will get dressed up no matter where they are heading - even if they're sightseeing in the Vatican or browsing elegant shops in Via Borgognona.

A long weekend can be enough to explore Rome's main sights, but a week will allow you to take your time and enjoy its surrounding areas. The main tourist season starts at Easter and runs until October. Peak periods are during Spring and Autumn, when tour buses pour in and tourists are herded around. If you do visit in summer, try to hit the sights in the morning, take a long lunch or a dip in your hotel pool during the afternoon, and then head out again around 6 pm for a meal and perhaps a fresh *gelato* (*ice cream*) to take advantage of the cooler evenings. Walking is perhaps the easiest way to get around, although if you plan on staying outside the city centre then a taxi is often the most convenient.

Opposite page. Looking down from spanish steps in Rome.

It's difficult to forget about Rome's rich history - there are reminders at almost every corner. The Colosseum is arguably the most thrilling of all of Rome's monuments. The hordes of visitors who queue to get in are testaments to its appeal. The blockbuster film 'Gladiator', starring Russell Crowe, was filmed in the Colosseum, which may have increased its popularity, especially among Americans.

The amphitheatre was constructed in AD 72 by Emperor Vespasian. It had an original capacity of 50,000 spectators and it showcased mortal combats between gladiators and fights between condemned prisoners and wild animals (including crocodiles, bears, tigers, elephants and hippos). With the fall of the Roman Empire, the Colosseum was abandoned and became overgrown with exotic plants from seeds which had accidentally been transported with the wild beasts. Earthquakes caused further damage to the Colosseum, and to this day it remains an evocative place to explore.

Via del Corso, Rome's main thoroughfare, cuts through the length of the city centre. It starts at Piazza Venezia in the South, runs past the vast marble Vittorio Emanuele Monument (which was erected to commemorate the unification of Italy and honor her first king), to emerge in Piazza del Popolo in the North. Beyond here lies the cool green refuge of the Villa Borghese, where you can observe skate-boarders, explore some wonderful greenery, or gawk at private art collections at the Borghese Gallery and Museum. The collections at this gallery were formed by Cardinal Scipione Borghese, the most passionate and knowledgeable art collector of his era. The collection includes works by Caravaggio, Bernini, Botticelli and Raphael.

East of Via del Corso lie elegant shopping streets, including Via Borgognona and Via Condotti, where you will find refined Italian and international fashion designers launching their collections. If you are visiting during the summer, don't forget that most shops close for *siesta* in mid-afternoon. But shops do open in the early evening - a little retail therapy in the evening before heading out for dinner is a wonderful experience.

Adventure: City Slicker
Destination: Rome

Via Borgognona leads to Piazza di Spagna (at the bottom of the famous Spanish Steps). Here you will see a myriad of tourists who come here often just to sit on the steps and soak up the atmosphere, while street sellers and caricature artists work at the foot of the steps.

The Spanish Steps (Scalinata della Trinita' dei Monti) are a majestic series of steps which lead up to an impressive church, the Chiesa di Trinita' dei Monti. The best view of this complex is from far down Via Condotti. At certain times during early summer, the steps are covered with pots of colourful flowers, making a delightful sight. However, early summer is also the busiest time for tourists, so it's unlikely that the steps will be empty at this time of year.

At the nearby Trevi Fountain, Rome's largest and most famous fountain, there is a tradition for visitors to drop a coin into the water to guarantee their return to Rome. A second coin will have you falling in love with an Italian, and a third means you will marry him or her.

To the west of Via del Corso there is a maze of narrow streets which winds its way down to the River Tiber. It is these narrow streets, in the historic centre of Rome, that the most complete ancient Roman structure is found - the Pantheon. The structure was completed in AD 125 by Emperor Hadrian. The diameter of the dome and its height are precisely equal, while its interior is illuminated by sunlight which enters through a hole in the dome's roof which is 9.1 metres in diameter.

Across the River Tiber is the Vatican City. This is the smallest independent state in the world, in terms of population and area. The Vatican is filled with inspiring gardens and also contains St Peter's Basilica, Castle Gandolfo and the Vatican palaces.

St Peter's Basilica, at the centre of the Vatican City, is the largest religious building in the world. The basilica was erected over the tomb of St Peter the Apostle and is the fruit of the combined genius of Bramante, Raphael, Michelangelo, Bernini and Maderna. Vatican jurisdiction covers the Vatican city, as well as some areas within and outside Rome.

Moving south, the district of Trastevere offers an alternative focus. The district is home to numerous bars, restaurants and nightclubs. One of the main tourist attractions in this area is the Bocca Della Verita (Mouth of Truth), a 2,500 year old image which has been carved from Pavonazzetto marble. Located in the atrium of the church of Santa Maria in Cosmedin, the mysterious plaque is thought to be part of an ancient Roman fountain or manhole cover, portraying one of several possible pagan gods. The most famous characteristic of the mouth, however, is its role as a lie detector. Since the Middle Ages, it has been believed that if you tell a lie with your hand in its mouth it will be bitten off!

Below left. Outside the Exedra.
Below right. Pizzeria da Baffeto, the best
pizza in town.

ꙮ Stylish Places to Stay

Lavish Style: Exedra. Situated on the Piazza della
Repubblica and owned by exclusive Italian hotel
group Boscolo, Exedra epitomises modern Italian
style and glamour. The rooms are decorated in
calming and subtle colours, and there are plasma
screen TVs in the bathrooms. Breakfast includes
every imaginable type of pastry, meat, cheese and
coffee. Most importantly, the views from the rooftop
pool are to die for. ⭐

Pampering Style: Es Hotel. Centrally located
right next to the Terminus train station and within
walking distance to many historic sites, this modern
hotel has been recently acquired by the Radisson
group. It is famous for extravagant cocktails served
by the rooftop pool, as well as for being a hangout
for various Oceans Twelve actors during filming. ⭐

Cool Arty Style: Hotel Art. This luxury boutique
hotel is located near Piazza di Spagna, an ideal
position for the best designer shopping in Rome -
on Via Babuino and Via Dei Condotti - and the
antiquarian shops of Via Margutta. Room designs
are cutting-edge and have all the latest hi-tech
equipment. The gym includes a Turkish steam bath.

ꙮ Delicious Places to Eat

Courtyard Chic: Gusto Restaurant. This
restaurant is made up of two separate parts.
The simpler and more informal of the two is a
street-level pizzeria, where a dozen kinds of
homemade pasta and pizza are offered, along with
freshly made salads and simple platters of such
grilled specialities as veal, chicken, steak and fish.
More upscale, and somewhat calmer, is the
upstairs restaurant, where big windows, high
ceilings, floors of glowing hardwood and lots of
exposed brick create an appropriately minimalist
setting for cutting-edge cuisine. You can also opt
to sit outside and dine *al fresco*. ⭐

Perfect Traditional Pizzas: Pizzeria Da Baffetto.
Located down a side street, Pizzeria da Baffetto is
a Roman institution. The wood-burning oven lets off
the aroma of mozzarella and fresh basil. Its large,
excellent-value pizzas would feed an army and
deserve their reputation as among the best in Rome.
Expect to join a queue if you arrive after 9 pm, and
don't be surprised if you end up sharing a table.

Romantic: Imago Hassler Hotel. Located on
the sixth floor of the Hassler hotel, this is one
of the most romantic spots for a candlelit dinner
with stunning views of the city's historic sites,
including St Peter's Basilica. Its cuisine is as
exquisite as its service is impeccable. Save this
one for a special occasion!

Adventure: Culture Vulture
Destination: Florence

✈ Regional Information

Florence, the capital of Tuscany, is set deep in rolling countryside and is steeped in history, atmosphere and culture. Visitors to Florence are always amazed by the sheer number of striking attractions, such as wonderful buildings, Renaissance art galleries, treasure-crammed museums, fine churches and enormous palaces. It's a culture vulture's haven and is perfect for a long weekend, or a week if you wish to explore the tree-lined countryside of Tuscany.

The city centre is fairly compact - many of its chief attractions are consolidated in a few areas - so the main highlights are accessible on foot. In fact, it is possible for pedestrians to traverse the city centre in approximately half an hour, although this assumes that they don't stop to gaze at the awe-inspiring sights.

Florence is served by two large airports, Pisa International Airport (Galileo Galilei) and Florence Airport (Amerigo Vespucci), both of which are within easy reach of the city centre.

The Medici family, a powerful an influential Florentine family from the 13th to the 17th century, had a significant bearing on the appearance of Florence. The family commissioned the construction of grand buildings, town squares and superb gardens. One example is the town mansion - Palazzo Medici-Riccardi on Via Cavour - where the family resided until 1540 with its famous Renaissance façade. Over the years, this palace has been home for countless famous individuals, including Italian royalty and artists. Across the road are the stunning Medici Chapels, which were built to serve as mausoleums to the family, illustrating their immense wealth and influence.

Florence is built around a large river, the Arno, which has can be crossed by bridge at many points. But, without doubt, the grandest of all the bridges is Ponte Vecchio (Old Bridge), which was built in 1345. This three-arched bridge is the oldest bridge in Florence and is lined with shops - mostly jewellers and goldsmiths. High above the shops is a secret passageway, which links the Uffizi Gallery to the Pitti Palace, and this is now open to the public.

Many of Italy's most famous artists, including Michelangelo, Donatello and Leonardo Da Vinci, had a hand in designing and creating many of Florence's most impressive buildings. For example, Brunelleschi's revolutionary design for the Basilica di Santa Maria del Fiore - also known as the Duomo - is generally accepted as the first expression of Renaissance ideas in architecture. The Duomo is the fourth largest Cathedral in the world and, as such, dominates the city's skyline. Similarly, the great Piazza del Duomo at the foot of the Duomo dominates life at street level. The *piazza* (square) is ringed with cafés and is a popular meeting point for locals and tourists. Between there and the river are many of the best-loved *palazzi* (palaces), whilst close by to the north are the churches of San Lorenzo and Santa Maria Novella - one of the most important Gothic churches in Tuscany.

Florence's galleries will keep any art enthusiast busy for days. The Uffizi Gallery houses one of the world's most celebrated art collections, which includes works such as Botticelli's *Birth Of Venus*, Caravaggio's *Young Bacchus*, Leonardo da Vinci's *Annunciation*, Michelangelo's *Holy family* and Titian's *Urbino Venus*. For fans of sculpture, the Museo Nazionale del Bargello offers notable works by Michelangelo and Donatello. Also, Michelangelo's famous statue of *David* may be viewed at the Accademia di Belle Arti near the University.

The Palazzo Pitti, situated on the southern bank of the River Arno, features wonderful pieces of art by Raphael, Filippo Lippi, Tintoretto, Veronese and Rubens. The palace is also home to a modern art collection and a costume collection. Outside, to the rear, is one of Florence's top tourist attractions - the stunning landscaped Boboli Gardens. These gardens feature ponds, fountains and formal clipped hedges.

Florence's town hall, the Palazzo Vecchio, was completed in 1322. Its tall and imposing bell tower was built to announce city meetings or to warn of flood, fire or attack. Much of its interior was remodelled by Georgio Vasari, who created a number of elaborate and decorative features, when Duke Cosimo I moved into the palace in 1540. Despite this remodelling the building still retains a fairly medieval appearance.

The Piazza della Signoria is a truly unique outdoor sculpture gallery. It is surrounded by some of the city's most celebrated buildings and has the reputation of being the hub of the city's politics since the 14th century. Indeed, many striking statues commemorate important political events in the city's history.

Adventure: Culture Vulture
Destination: Florence

Basilica di Santa Croce was built in 1385. It is as much a resting place of late Florentine geniuses as it is a repository of stunning art. It is located near the National Library.

Several artists' tombs can be found here, including that of Michelangelo, Galileo and composer Rossini. The two chapels of the Bardi and Peruzzi clans are decorated frescoes by Giotto. The basilica is perfect for a Sunday afternoon stroll.

Palazzo Strozzi is one of the most magnificent palaces in the city. Located near to 'Piazza Della Repubblica', it was built in 1536 for a wealthy banker, Filippo Strozzi, who died just two years after the foundations had been laid. The palace is three storeys high and each floor is as tall as a normal *palazzo*. Today, the palace is used for art exhibitions and also houses various institutes and a large library.

The Palazzo dei Congressi is the best exhibition and modern international conference centre in Florence. The centre is housed in an 18th-century villa, a renaissance style building with outstanding period furnishings. Situated next to Santa Maria Novella, the conference centre offers superb facilities for large events, including 13 rooms and an open-air amphitheatre. Its beautifully landscaped gardens offer visitors a wonderful haven of tranquility and an opportunity to escape the tourists.

Near to the Piazza Vittorio Veneto is the Teatro del Maggio Musicale Fiorentino (previously known as Teatro Comunale), the most important concert hall in the city. Over the years, countless famous names have performed on this stage, such as Maria Callas, Richard Strauss, Igor Stravinsky, Luciano Berio and many others. The main theatre area can seat around 2,000 people. There are many concerts, operas, festivals and events held in this theatre throughout the year, including the famous Maggio Musicale Fiorentino - a lovely evening out for lovers of music.

Opposite page, Left. Relais La Suvera.
Right. Ristorante Beccofino.

Modern Art Style: Una Hotel Vittoria. Located in the residential quarter of San Frediano, this hotel offers the latest in style, design and technology. Vibrant colours and rare materials such as mosaics, leather and printed fabrics have been used in all rooms, which are also fitted with plasma screens mounted on pink sparkly walls. If you are sharing a room, make sure you know them well, as all and bathrooms have clear glass screens which are completely transparent.

Luxury Charm: JK Place. This hotel, just a few steps away from Ponte Vecchio, has a real homely feel with fireplaces aglow, contemporary colours and an attentive service. With only 20 rooms, it feels like an exclusive members' club. Opt for the penthouse suite with stunning views of Florence from a private terrace.

Rural Retreat: Relais la Suvera. Located in the small hamlet of Pievescole, Relais la Suvera is a real retreat. Its tranquil setting with an aviary, private chapel and great views of the Tuscan countryside, is only an hour away from Florence centre. Every room is filled with unique pieces of art from the Family's extensive collection of antiques, married with modern marble bathrooms and butler service. The homemade breakfasts are delicious. ✪

Tuscan Modern: Ristorante Beccofino. Chef Berardinelli creates delightful and innovative Tuscan dishes in a sleek modern surrounding. In the summer you can enjoy your meal on an outdoor terrace overloooking the Arno Beccofino. The restaurant's also a hot spot for young Florentines. Staff are smooth and courteous, the soundtrack is groovy and there's a superb list of wines.

Gourmet Renaissance: Enoteca Pinchiorri. Owned by Relais & Chateaux, this Michelin-starred restaurant is set in a frescoed Renaissance palace, where the owner himself helps you choose your wine from his unique 150,000-bottle cellar. Dress code is smart and men must wear a jacket and tie.

Descreet & Local: Cibreo. Tucked away in the heart of the historic district of Santa Croce, this beautifully kept restaurant's old-fashioned charm and flair for local cuisine have made it a popular haunt. The food is fantastic - from the creamy *crostini di fegatini* (a savory chicken liver spread) to the melt-in-your-mouth desserts. Chef Fabio Picchi's boasts that his food is among the best and most creative in town.

Adventure: Rest + Relaxation
Destination: Amalfi Coast

⚓ Regional Information

The Amalfi coast, which runs from Sorrento to Salerno, is one of Europe's most beautiful and romantic shores. The entire coastline is a great destination for travellers looking for a relaxing romantic retreat.

For 50 km the bendy road hugs the rugged coastline and overlooks intense blue waters, picture postcard villages and villas which seem to cling to the cliff walls like matchbox houses. The towns of Amalfi, Positano and Ravello, offer lush flora, superb cuisine, fine wine, excellent historic sites and spectacular scenery. You can also find great souvenirs and wonderful gastronomic delights, such as giant lemons, *limoncello* (the local lemon liqueur), and *mozzarella di bufala*. The nearby island of Capri is one of Italy's most celebrated areas of beauty.

In getting to the Amalfi coast, most visitors will fly directly into Naples airport and either hire a car or grab a taxi. Hiring a car is the best option if you want to explore the sites and scenery independently. But be careful - the hairpin bends and narrow roads can make driving a nerve-racking experience for even the most experienced of drivers. Note that driving and parking in some smaller towns, for example in Ravello, are prohibited. A week should be long enough to explore the area, relax and enjoy the sights.

Naples, the third-largest city in Italy, is famous for being the city where the pizza was invented. Set on the Bay of Naples and overshadowed by Mount Vesuvius, Naples occupies one of the most beautiful natural settings of any city in Europe. Although it is frequently criticised for its social problems - such as urban decay, delinquency and littered streets - it still has several cultural attractions which are worth visiting.

Notable monuments in Naples include: the 17th century Palazzo Real; the massive stone Castel Nuovo overlooking the sea; and the San Carlo Opera House. In addition, the impressive Museo Archeologico Nazionale houses an excellent collection of Greco-Roman artifacts, including mosaics from Pompeii and Herculaneum.

Perhaps one of the most alluring aspects of Naples is its proximity to Mount Vesuvius; it is possible to explore Mount Vesuvius during the day and be back in the city for dinner. Mount Vesuvius is one of Europe's active volcanos. It towers above the Bay of Naples and the Tyrrhennian Sea and is inevitably one of the area's leading attractions. Since it exploded in AD 79, burying Pompeii, Herculaneum and much of the surrounding countryside, Vesuvius has erupted more than 30 times, most recently in 1944. Nowadays, daily observation is carried out to assess any movement or activity. Visitors can walk to the summit rim and peer into the giant 7 km-wide crater. If you choose to ascend the volcano, you will need to wear comfortable walking shoes, and the helpful old man at the entrance point will give you a walking stick if you want one. The best viewing platform is on the rim. It provides a good view of the steam filled abyss as well as the whole of the Bay of Naples.

Nearby, the remains of the town of Pompeii are a unique record of how Romans lived their daily lives during the 1st century BC. At Pompeii, visitors can see moulds and fossils of people and animals which are extremely well-preserved. The decoration in some of the excavated villas is amazingly intact, including numerous wall paintings of gods and humans in scenes ranging from the heroic to the erotic. Pompeii is Europe's most compelling archaeological site. The town has been kept preserved for over 2,000 years by volcanic pumice from Mount Vesuvius. Pompeii covers an area of 66 hectares of land (only 44 hectares have been excavated) so visitors will need at least a full day to fully explore the ruins. An audio guide is available for hire near the entrance point at Porta Marina and is definitely a worthwhile investment if you are visiting without a tour guide.

Adventure: Rest + Relaxation
Destination: Amalfi Coast

Capri, one of Italy's most beautiful and most visited islands, can be reached by ferry or hydrofoil from Amalfi, Naples, Positano or Sorrento.

In addition to wonderful beaches and shops, the main attractions of Capri include: a trip to Ischia, a volcanic island which is great for mineral springs and spas (the hydrofoil takes just 20 minutes from Capri); the Marina Grande, the island's main port; the Blue Grotto, a famous sea cave (requires a short boat trip to get there); the ruins of Villa Tiberio, built as the Roman Emperor Tiberius's luxurious retirement home (requires a strenuous 45 minute uphill treck); and the pretty but crowded Garden of Augustus, south of the town of Capri.

Capri is a shopping heaven for those who love designer brands - you can buy everything from Dolce & Gabbanna stilettos to Louis Vuitton handbags. Capri has long been a famous haunt for the rich and famous, and the prices really reflect it. It's great for a day's visit from the mainland or a few days' stay.

Back on the mainland, Positano is perhaps one of the coast's most picturesque towns. There is everything a visitor could want: crumbling walls steeped in history, boats bobbing on the small marina at Spiaggia Grande, not to mention the town's most attractive building, the Chiesa di Santa Maria Assunta - a picturesque church with broken pillars and winged cherubs.

The town's narrow colourful streets, gorgeous quaint hotels, warm hospitality and wonderfully laid back pace of life make it an ideal destination for a relaxing evening meal or a few quiet drinks.

Amalfi is perhaps the most well known resort town in the region. Despite its popularity with tourists the town still has an authentic air. The Romanesque cathedral, located in the main square, has a 13th century bell tower and looks untouched by the hustle and bustle which surround it. The Cloister of Paradise, just to the right of the cathedral, also makes good viewing. There are some excellent restaurants and the local wine, Sammarco, bottled in Amalfi, is superb and inexpensive.

The most spectacular views of the Amalfi Coast can be had from the town of Ravello, a former independent republic which is ideal for a day trip. The town is perched 335 metres above sea level, high above Amalfi, and was once described by French author André Gide as being 'closer to the sky than the seashore'. To enjoy these views, head to the Villa Cimbrone, where marble statues line a belvedere which is perched on the very edge of a cliff. Ravello is also famous for its annual music festival and ravishing gardens.

The town is certainly one of the best locations on the coastline for a romantic stopover, offering extremely luxurious hotels, relaxing walks, and excellent local cuisine. It's so romantic that many couples decide to get married there and, during the summer, there can be as many as three or four weddings a week.

Top. Palazzo Sasso, Ravello.
Bottom. Le Sirenuse, Postiano.

ꜗ Stylish Places to Stay

Romantic Style: Palazzo Sasso. Set in the charming town of Ravello, this hotel has everything for those wanting romance, luxury, seclusion and tranquility. As a former 12th century palace, it offers incredible views, an unbelievable Michelin 2-star restaurant, and a gorgeous spa. ⭐ ⭐

Artistic Style: Casa Angelina. Casa Angelina in Priano offers the luxury and comfort of a five star hotel in an artistic and charming atmosphere. Sheltered on a cliff overlooking the Mediterranean Sea, the hotel provides all that lovers of the sea and tranquillity are looking for.

Sumptuous Style: Capri Palace. Located in Ana Capri and situated 300 meters above sea level, this hotel offers spectacular views of the Gulf of Naples. Deluxe style at its best - you won't want to leave.

⭑ Delicious Places to Eat

Local Charm: Cumpa Cosimo. On entering this restaurant in Ravello, the delightful hostess, Netta Bottone, welcomes you into her family as though you have lived here for years. The restaurant has been in operation for 3 centuries and everything is locally produced. The *funghi porcini* mushroom starter and the house cheesecake are so delicious you'll drop your fork. Local wines ease it all down gently, and homemade *gelato* is a luscious ending. ⭐

Italian Chic: Le Sirenuse. Evening champagne cocktails are a must on the Oyster Bar terrace at Le Sirenuse as the sun sets in Positano. Evening dinner is quite formal, which provides a great excuse for dressing up to be waited on hand and foot. ⭐

Hidden Gem: Buca di Bacco. This delightful little restaurant is hidden away in the heart of the historic centre of Capri. Guests dine in rooms with the characteristic vaulted ceilings of the island's oldest buildings, in a structure built on the ruins of ancient Greek walls. Fantastic views over the deep blue sea.

Focus On...
Cinque Terre

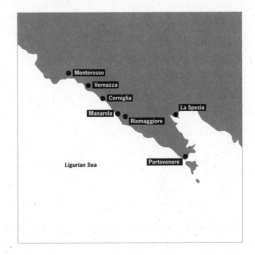

Cinque Terre (or 'five lands') is a national park and a UNESCO protected territory with naturalistic environmental interest. It is made up of five villages - Monterosso, Vernazza, Corniglia, Manarola and Riomaggiore - which are all on the coast.

Each village consists of cliff sides that are covered by terraced vineyards and countless dry-stone walls which lie precipitously to the sea. Wine growers use monorail mechanisms to get up to their vineyards and to bring their grapes down to the village. Olive groves can be found on the lower slopes. The area is so beautiful that tourism overtook fishing and viniculture as the main local industry a long time ago.

Cinque Terre offers some beautiful scenic walks, some of which are simple and others that are physically challenging. The Via Dell'Amore, or Lovers' Way, is a path from Riomaggiore to Manarola. This path follows the coastline and is therefore very picturesque, but it varies in difficulty from an easy stroll to a rough and physically challenging hike.

The stretch from Manarola to Corniglia is easy to hike and takes about 30 minutes, although the main trail into Corniglia finishes with a climb of more than 300 steps and takes about an hour. The trail from Corniglia to Vernazza is steep in places but the trail from Vernazza to Monterosso is by far the steepest part and both sections can get rough in places. It will take you an hour and a half to get from Corniglia to Monterosso, but the strain is worth it. The path winds through countless olive groves and vineyards and the biggest reward is the view of the bay and the spectacular approaches to both Monterosso and Vernazza. Just one word of warning, there are nominal fees to use the more popular walking trails, and parking can be very difficult during peak times, especially at weekends.

If you'd prefer to visit the villages by boat you buy a boat pass from the departure point at the town of La Spezia. If you want to spend a few days exploring the five villages you can leave your car at La Spezia and find a hotel in one of the villages.

Opposite page. Cinque Terre - Vernazza.

ⓘ Stylish Essentials

General Tourist Information

National Tourist Office
Via Marghera 2
00185
www.enit.it
T. +39 06 4 97 11 (info)

Tourist Information
www.italiantourism.com

Embassies

U.K. Embassy
Via Settembre 80A
Rome
T. +39 06-422-00001

U.K. Consulate in Florence
Via Lungarno Corsini 2
Florence
T. +39 055-284-133

Consulate General in Naples
Via Dei Mille 40
Naples
T. +39 081-4238-911

Airlines

Alitalia
www.alitalia.com
T. 08714 241 424 (UK reservations)

BA
www.ba.com

BMI
www.flybmi.com

Meridiana
www.meridiana.it
T. 0845 3555588 (UK Reservations)

Ryan Air
www.ryanair.com

Easyjet
www.easyjet.co.uk

Thomsonfly
www.thomsonfly.com

Rail Travel
www.raileurope.com

Rome

Rome Airports (Ciampino and Fiumicino)
www.adr.it/

General information
General information on the city of Rome from multilingual personnel
T. +39 06 3600 4399

Colosseum
Piazza del Colosseo
www.pierreci.it
T. +39 06 39 96 77 00 (info)
Open: Ticket office 8.30 am – 6.15 pm

Museo e Galleria Borghese
Piazzale del Museo Borghese
www.ticketeria.it
T. +39 06 32 81 01 (info)
Open: Tue-Sun 9:00am-7:00pm

Pantheon
Piazza della Rotonda
T. +39 06 683 00 230 (info)

The Vatican
www.vatican.va

Boscolo Exedra Hotel
www.boscolohotels.com
T. +39 06 421 111

Es Hotel
www.rome.radissonsas.com
T. +39 06 444841

Hotel Art
www.hotelartrome.com
T. +39 06 32 8711

Gusto Restaurant
Piazza Augusto Imeratore 9, Tridente
T. +39 06 322 6273

Pizzeria da Baffetto
Via del Governo Vecchio ,11
T. +39 066861611

Hotel Hassler Roma – Restaurant
6th Floor
Trinità dei Monti 600187 Roma – Italia
www.hotelhasslerroma.com
T. 39 06 699 34 428

Florence

Pisa International Airport Galileo
Galilei
www.pisa-airport.com

Palazzo Medici-Riccardi
Via Cavour 11, Florence

Palazzo Vecchio (Old Palace)
Piazza della Signoria,
T. +39 055 276 82 24 (info)

Duomo
www.operaduomo.firenze.it
T. +39 055 230 28 85 (info)
Open: Mon-Wed, Fri 10:00am-5:00pm,
Thu 10:00am-3:30pm, Sat 10:00am-
4:45pm, Sun 1:00pm-4:45pm

Basilica di Santa Croce
Piazza di Santa Croce 16
T. +39 055 246 61 05 (info)
Open: Mon-Sat 9:00am-5:30pm;
Sun 1:00pm-5:30pm

Galleria degli Uffizi
Piazzale degli Uffizi 6
www.polomuseale.firenze.it/uffizi
T. +39 055 238 86 51 (info)
Open: Tue-Sun 8:15am-6:50pm

Palazzo Pitti
Piazza de' Pitti
T. +39 055 238 86 14 (info)
Open: Mar 8:15am-5:30pm; Apr-May
& Sep-Oct 8:15am-6:30pm

Palazzo dei Congressi
14 Viale Filippo Strozzi,

Teatro del Maggio Musicale
Fiorentino.
16, Corso Italia
www.maggiofiorentino.com
(also in English)

JK Place
www.jkplace.com
T. +39 055 2645181

Una Hotel Vittoria
www.unahotels.it
T. +39 055 22771

Relais La Suvera
www.lasuvera.it
T. +39 0577 960300

Ristorante Beccofino
Piazza degli Scarlatti 1/r
www.truetuscany.com/food/rest/
beccofino.shtml
T. +39 055 29 00 76 (info)
E. baldovino.beccofino@inwind.it

Enoteca Pinchiorri
Via Ghibellina, 87
www.enotecapinchiorri.com
T. +39 055 242 777
Closes: Sunday, Monday, Tuesday
noon and Wednesday noon

Cibero
Via A. del Verrocchio 8/r,
Florence, Italy
T. +39 055 2341100
Closed Sun. and Mon.

Amalfi Coast

Capodichino airport
www.gesac.it
T. +39 081 789 6259

General Visitor Information
www.ravellotime.it
www.amalfitouristoffice.it
www.positano.com
www.anacapri-life.com
www.capri.net
www.capritourism.com

Amalfi Coast Private Transfers
T. +39 334 330 21 92
E. res@easycoast.com

Private Boats to Capri
www.romanticboat.it
T. +39 320.2827087
E. info@romanticboat.it

Alilauro
www.alilaurogruson.it
T. +39 081/5513882 or
081/8376995

Linee Marittime Partenopee
www.consorziolmp.it
T. +39 081 8781430 or
081 8071812

Metro del Mare
www.metrodelmare.com

Navigazione Libera Del Golfo
www.navlib.it/index.asp
T. +39 081 5527209 hydrofoils
from Naples;
T. +39 089 875092 ferry and
hydrofoils from Positano,

SNAV
www.snav.it
T. +39 081/7612348 or
081/8377577

Mount Vesuvios
www.parconazionaledelvesuvio.it
www.vesuvioinrete.it/e_parco.htm
Open: 9.00am - 6.00pm

Pompeii
Entrance Porta Marina, Piazza
Anfiteatro
T. +39 081 857 53 47 (Ticket Office)
Open: 08.30 - 19.30

Ravello Music Festival
www.ravellofestival.com

Palazzo Sasso (Ravello)
www.palazzosasso.com
T. +39 089 818181

Casa Angelina (Priano)
www.casangelina.com
T. +39 089 813 13 33

Capri Palace (Ana Capri)
www.capripalace.com
T. +39 081 978 0111

Cumpa Cosimo (Ravello)
Via Roma, Ravello
T. +39 089 85 7156
Closed Mondays Nov-Feb open
daily Mar-Oct

Le Sirenuse (Positano)
Via C.Colombo, 30
84017 Positano
www.sirenuse.it
T. +39 089 87 50 66
E. info@sirenuse.it

Buca di Bacco (Capri)
Via Longano, 35
80073 Capri
T. +39 081 8370723
E. enminier@tin.it

Focus on Cinque Terre

Tourist Information
www.cinqueterre.it

Boat Pass around Cinque Terre
www.navigazionegolfodeipoeti.it

Yellow cab in New York City.

ONE WAY

NO
TURNS

W 43 ST

ONE

cingular
WIRELESS

4H84E

USA

New York City | Los Angeles |
Las Vegas & Grand Canyon | Miami

HOLLYWOOD

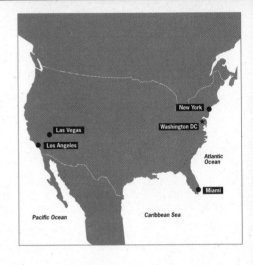

Why is this place so special?

You could spend all of your life travelling through the USA and you would still probably wouldn't be able to see everything the country has to offer. It's a massive place and is home to some of the world's most exciting cities, long white beaches, truly mind-blowing landscapes, diverse geography, and the most approachable natives in the world. Folks, welcome to America.

The USA is sometimes referred to as 'The Land of Opportunity' and there are certainly a huge number of opportunities for travel. Really, the USA is like several countries rolled into one. It is a country that offers an abundance of geographic diversity and the climate ranges from tropical to arctic.

Some examples of activities for travellers include: wandering city streets, partying till dawn, horse riding through the desolate Grand Canyon, lazing on beaches, becoming starry-eyed watching movies being filmed. All over the country there are various national parks which are great for hiking, biking and other activities. Yellowstone, Yosemite, and the Grand Canyon are particularly well known national parks.

The global distribution of American movies and TV shows has shaped the world's perception of the country to a high, if not entirely accurate, degree. Most travellers have some kind of perception of America before they visit. Los Angeles is sometimes believed to be a 'land of make-believe', so many travellers tend to gravitate towards this city to catch a glimpse of the legendary Hollywood sign or take a tour of the star's extensive homes.

Sport plays an important role in American society. It has developed rapidly and separately from the rest of the world's sporting activities. Consequently, homegrown games such as baseball, American football (not the British kind), ice hockey and basketball dominate the country's sport scene. Urban America also invented the great 'indoors' - aerobics at the gym, indoor skiing and indoor rock climbing. So, wherever you are and whatever time it is, you will be able to observe or play a sport of some kind.

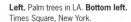

Left. Palm trees in LA. **Bottom left.** Times Square, New York.

Some of the world's best (and most famous) beaches can be found in the USA. Long, white stretches of sand line the sunny Californian coastline, from Venice beach to Santa Monica and beyond, where swimmers are watched by scantily clad lifeguards. Nightclubs and swish hotels line the coast of South Beach in Miami, Florida, where the locals party from night to dawn and plastic surgery is an epidemic.

Whether you are taking a road trip expedition, gambling to your heart's content, or spending until your credit cards are maxed-out, the USA offers it all.

Fast Facts

Capital: Washington DC.

Location: The USA is made up of 50 states, 1 federal state, and 14 territories. It borders Canada to the north and Mexico to the south. Alaska juts out from northwestern Canada and Hawaii lies 2,500 miles off the west coast in the middle of the Pacific.

Population: 290,000,000.

Religion: Protestant (50%), Roman Catholic (25%), Jewish (2%), Muslim (1%).

Language: American English is the official main language. Spanish has effective dual-language status in parts of Southern California, New Mexico, Texas and Miami. There are also 400,000 speakers of Native American dialects.

✈ Getting there and exploring around

Getting to the USA shouldn't be a problem. Many airlines fly directly from the UK to most major cities, including New York, Las Vegas, LA, Miami, Boston, Washington, Chicago, Seattle and San Francisco. Silverjet and Maxijet offer direct business-only flights to New York with larger seats and more legroom.

There are also plenty of efficient overland border crossings between the USA and Canada and Mexico - you have the option of driving, catching a bus or an Amtrak train.

If you have a UK or British Passport then a 90-day visitor's visa will be issued upon arrival either at the border crossing or at the customs desk at the airport. The USA is regularly adjusting entry requirements in an effort to reduce the threat of terrorism. It is imperative that travellers double-check current regulations before coming to the USA, as changes are likely to occur without warning. A procedure which was introduced in 2004 requires most visitors travelling on visas to the United States to have two fingerprints scanned by an inkless device and a digital photograph taken by immigration officials upon entry at US air and seaports.

Once you're inside the USA, there are many options for domestic travel. Air travel is the most common form of domestic travel - there are lots of domestic airlines, so competition on popular routes and frequent discounting makes flying within the US a relatively inexpensive option (though fares can be higher on less popular routes).

Trains and bus services between major cities and states are long, tiresome and not very comfortable.

Exploring the USA by car is a far more practical and exciting option. Exploring the USA by car is so easy: the highway system is excellent, signage will tell you where the attractions are, at all major interchanges there are hotels, motels, restaurants and gas stations to help you in your travels and the tourist attractions are just endless wherever you go. Rental cars are plentiful and relatively cheap, though major agencies require you to be at least 25 years old.

Urban public transportation is generally quite good, catching the subway in New York or the El in Chicago are as integral a part of the American travelling experience as hopping on a double-decker bus in London. But nothing beats climbing into a huge stretch limo and arriving at your hotel in style. Many hotels offer this option free of charge (you just need to tip the driver).

Walking is considered a very un-American activity, unless it takes place on hiking trails in national parks. So when you ask someone directions and they say it's so far you need to get a cab, you could probably walk it in 5 minutes.

☞ Best time of year to visit

Being the fourth largest country in the world, America's weather is certain to be diverse. Compared with countries of Western Europe in the same latitude, the USA has greater extremes of temperature, and daily or weekly changes are more noticeable.

On occasion, parts of the USA experiences extremes of heat and cold characteristic of hot tropical deserts or cold Arctic continental regions. Another feature of the weather and climate is the variation of weather over quite short periods at all seasons of the year.

Some parts of the USA are liable to experience two particularly violent and destructive weather phenomena - hurricanes and tornadoes. Hurricanes affect the south eastern states which border the Gulf of Mexico and the Atlantic. These tropical storms, which bring very strong winds and torrential rainfall, originate in the warm waters of the Caribbean and head north east into the Gulf of Mexico, or north up America's Atlantic coast.

Generally, it gets hotter the further south you go, and seasonally more extreme the further north and inland you head from the coasts. Winter in the North East and the upper Mid-West can bring long periods below freezing, even though it's still warm enough to swim in Florida and Southern California.

? Must know before you go

Don't lock your case. When travelling to the USA, or even through it, the Transportation Security Agency (TSA) has full authority to invade your luggage. If it is padlocked, they will simply cut open your luggage. You can either leave you luggage unlocked, or buy one of the specialised locks recommended by the TSA, which they can access easily.

Half a portion please? Food portions in most restaurants across the USA tend to be on the large side, especially if you are used to more modest European-sized dishes. Ask for a small portion or share with a friend, it'll save you money and be less of a waste.

Show me the money. This culture is obsessed with tipping. Everyone tips everyone, from bellboys to hairdressers. It used to be a courteous 10% for good service, but not anymore, tips can range up to 50% of the final bill. The golden rule is only tip for good service and tip generously if you are going to return.

🎁 Highlights

Shopping in New York. From Fifth Avenue to SoHo, shopping has never been this good, with unique boutiques and enormous department stores.

Living the dream in LA. Los Angeles is a micro-universe. You can find everything from rags to riches, from Tinseltown to East LA.

Cowboy adventures in Grand Canyon. Herd up the horses or ride alone in the desert and sleep under the stars.

Welcome to Miami. One of the most popular international tourist destinations in the world. Known for its Latin culture, never-ending nightlife, beautiful beaches and endless plastic surgery.

Adventure: City Slicker
Destination: New York City

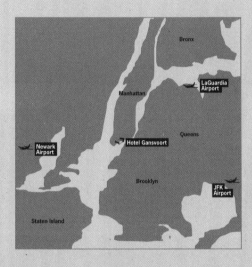

New York City is like a small universe - cities don't come much bigger than this one. When you walk between the high skyscrapers you feel small, and let's face it - you are. New York is densely packed with all types of nationalities, cultures and religions - making it one of the world's most impressive melting pots. It's hard to put a finger on what makes the place buzz so much, but its hyperactive rush keeps drawing more and more people to it. Among the main interests of New York City are the museums, the architecture and the endless shopping possibilities, especially along Fifth Avenue.

A week in New York is not long enough. In fact, it's difficult to estimate how much time spent in New York is enough. The city's array of attractions will make you a regular visitor. New York's most famous sights are Times Square, The Empire State Building and the Statue of Liberty.

Times Square is a neighbourhood in the borough of Manhattan which centres on 42nd Street and Broadway. It is named after the one-time headquarters of The New York Times newspaper. Feast your eyes on yellow cabs driving up and down, bustling tourists and brightly lit billboards. It's a great place for grabbing a late night coffee and watching the evening come to life.

The Empire State Building is a 102 storey building with a rich history - it represents a symbol of New York City all over the world. The Empire State Building stood as the tallest building in the world until 1972, when the World Trade Centre took the title. Nonetheless, it remains one of the most beloved and well recognised buildings in the world. Visitors can take the lift up to the top floor for some magnificent views across the city, which are best in the evening.

The Statue of Liberty, on Liberty Island, has to be seen by the naked eye in order for its beauty to be truly acknowledged. You can get to the island easily by ferry from Battery Park, and on a clear day, it offers great views over Manhattan. Even in her younger years this lovely tall lady welcomed people into New York Harbor and into America and she has always represented America's ideals of liberty and patriotism. The Statue of Liberty was a gift from the French to commemorate a long friendship between the two countries Visitors are only allowed to enter the pedestal and observational areas, although there is also a museum gallery. Be sure to allow yourself at least 2 hours for the trip from Battery Park.

In addition to these three main attractions, New York City has several districts that you should visit. Each one is distinctively different from the other.

Greenwich Village - if the winding streets of this historic neighbourhood could talk, they would speak of liberal politics and reform, such as poverty and prosperity, free love, socialism and gay rights. In Washington Square Park, you may catch a jam session in which anyone can participate.

Chinatown - New York's Chinatown is largest of its kind in the United States. It is located in one of the oldest neighbourhoods in Manhattan. Founded in the late 1870s by Chinese immigrants, Chinatown offers a unique historical and cultural experience not found anywhere else in the world. Recently, some non-Asian hotspots have opened in the district and these have created quite a stir.

Little Italy - just walk across Canal Street from Chinatown and you will feel like you are in Italy. The district offers Italian markets, Italian restaurants, Italian shops, and not least, a mass of Italian Americans.

Central Park - Manhattan's Central Park provides New Yorkers with a much-needed escape from the concrete, noise and traffic that is part of everyday life. What is perhaps most interesting about this 843 acre haven is that it is an entirely man-made park. Construction required 10 million cartloads of stone and earth to fill the area and over 500,000 trees and shrubs were planted here. Today, this plant life provides shelter to a surprising variety of wildlife. Check out the Central Park Wildlife Conservation Centre - home to over 100 species of animals from three different climate zones - the tropics, the polar circle, and the California coast.

Upper West Side - professionals, successful artists and apartment-sharing twenty somethings flock to this part of town. Today, the buildings along Central Park West house some extremely 'picky' celebrities (Jerry Seinfeld - approved; Madonna - denied). You can also find a thriving Jewish Orthodox singles scene. You cannot venture north of 90th Street on Amsterdam Avenue or Columbus Avenue without noticing it.

Broadway - a city slicker's trip wouldn't be complete without a visit to the Broadway district. You can see famous shows such as Cats, Phantom of the Opera, Hairspray and many others. Every season there is something special on show.

Adventure: City Slicker
Destination: New York City

Meatpacking District - This area owes its name to the meat distribution companies that once dominated the area. However, only a few meatpacking houses still exist today. Instead of meat packing, you are more likely to spot celebrities here, twirling around the Bermuda Triangle of SoHo House, Spice Market, Pastis and Hotel Gansevoort. Some art galleries have opened, but the area is dominated by late-night bars, high-end furniture stores, and fabulously expensive hairdressers. Head to this area at night if you are seeking a thrilling and pulsating nightlife with traffic jams building up over century-old cobblestones. If you would prefer to see the area when it is a little quieter, one of the most pleasant times of day to visit is between 10 and 11 o'clock in the morning.

A trip to New York is not complete without a day of shopping. Plan a stroll down Fifth Avenue, take your credit card and shop until you drop. Fifth Avenue department store takes elegant shopping to the extreme. The store offers a wonderful array of prestigious boutiques featuring top name designers. It's an experience for shoppers of all skill levels, and famous names include Saks, Gucci, Prada and Tiffany & Co.

Serious shoppers will also appreciate SoHo and Nolita (sometimes written NoLIta). Be warned though, there are so many different merchants it can be difficult to find the types of stores you want - even for the most committed and skilled shoppers!

You may be best to decide which stores you want to visit before you set off. Try Vintage New York for excellent wine (which is open on Sundays), American Apparel for ethical clothing or Apple's flagship store for some electrical gadgetry.

For those who wish to buy something other than clothes, check out witchcraft, candles, incense, books, music and magic at Enchantments, (mind the black cat). Or, if beautiful handicrafts are more your style, go to Clayworks Pottery on East Ninth Street.

↴ Stylish Places to Stay

Swanky Style: Gansvoort Hotel. Coated in zinc-coloured metal panels, the luxury Gansevoort's 14-storeys tower the above old meatpacking buildings. The hotel is one of Manhattan's hippest and the Meatpacking District is home to some of the most trendy boutiques, restaurants and clubs in the city. Opened in 2004, the Gansevoort is worth seeing even if you're not staying there. The rooftop bar, Plunge, draws block-long lines of well-dressed locals looking for a Hudson River view to accompany their martini. If you are a hotel resident you can jump the queue for the bar. ★

Exclusive Members-only: SoHo House. A former warehouse for electrical goods, the hotel shows off much of its industrial roots, with exposed beams and wooden floors and brick walls. The 'playpen' rooms are standard - quite small, but with a corner sofa, a metallic desk and creamy-green walls. Opt for a notch up: the 'playroom' with loftlike space, showers that double as steam rooms, automatic sliding curtains to split the room in two, and a snack drawer that includes 'naughty' oils.

Reading in Bed: Library Hotel. This hotel is in the heart of the city and has 60 themed rooms which are based on books. Guests may chose a topic and an associated room when they check in. It's slick, sultry and very unusual.

¶ Delicious Places to Eat

Stylish & Spicy: Spice Market. Considering its location (in the middle of the Meatpacking District), its ridiculous size (as big as a bus depot), and its strange hothouse décor, it's a wonder this restaurant works at all. But it does succeed very well. Sit at the cantilevered bar upstairs, where it's a pleasure to dine on chicken wings drizzled in a sticky-sweet chilli sauce, bowls of curried duck, or short ribs softened in a mass of onion and green chillies. Eat, drink and watch the party unfold.

French Patio Chic: Pastis. A French bistro in the heart of Manhattan's Meatpacking District. Pastis is open from breakfast to late-night supper and serves brunch at weekends. Restaurateur Keith McNally, whose other restaurants include Lucky Strike, Pravda and Balthazar, has created a traditional bistro which boasts a communal table for larger parties and an outdoor summer café. In summer, you will be astounded at how the streets become clogged with glitterati, limousines and gawkers. Fortunately the crowds have no impact on Pastis's quality of food. ★

Meathouse Mania: Macelleria Italian Steak House. This restaurant is a former meat warehouse with dangling meat hooks and carving tables to give the impression of a real life butchers shop. Not for vegetarians but perfect for devoted carnivores.

Adventure: Beach Bum
Destination: Los Angeles

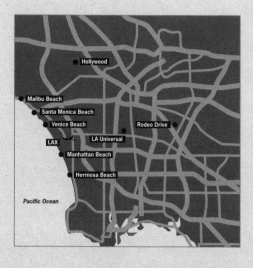

✦ Regional Information

'Fashion, film and famous beaches' usually sums up Los Angeles. Wannabe rock artists, film actors and hopeful starlets flock here every year 'try and make it' in the world of showbiz.

But there is a lot more to LA than just the Hollywood sign, Disneyland, and Baywatch babes.

LA is a glamorous metropolis with plenty of variety and year-round sunshine, which makes it a reliable choice for families, couples and solo travellers. Its highlights include Malibu and Laguna Beach, Mexican markets, Hawaiian sports, theme parks, chic shopping, celeb-spotting, dozens of ethnic neighbourhoods, Sunset Strip (also known as 'The Strip') and leafy Griffith Park. A few days are usually enough to explore the centre and outskirts, while a week is even better to explore LA's beaches and the surrounding vast mountain ranges.

One of the most exciting ways to get to LA is to take a road trip down the Pacific Coast Highway from San Francisco. It is a wonderful scenic route down the West coast, and is especially good fun if you can take your time.

However, most visitors find air travel the most convenient. LA has six airports - more than any other city in the world! Once you're in LA, it's a relatively easy place to get to know. Whether you want to explore by a blacked-out limo, drive a Cadillac, or pick up one of the local tour buses, it won't take you long before you know the city like the back of your hand.

One of the major attractions of LA is its laid-back culture and its vast beaches. Almost all of LA's south west coastline has magnificent sandy beaches. Most are open until dusk and are staffed by lifeguards. If the image of Pamela Anderson or David Hasslehoff in a swimsuit doesn't lure you here, then the sheer variety of beaches will. From Manhattan Beach (where the 'Beach Boys' music was born) to Venice Beach (where muscles abound), there is a beach for every type of traveller. The following are some of the best.

Manhattan Beach - yuppies and beach bums flock here to show off their volleyball skills. The beach is the birthplace of beach volleyball and was a Beach Boys' hangout in the early days of their careers. It faces west and attracts a broad mix of visitors. An open volleyball championship takes place every August. There are also sand castle and surfing contests.

Dockweiler Beach - a three-mile-long section of Los Angeles shoreline that's seldom crowded. Dockweiler is the only place in Los Angeles County where you are legally allowed to have a bonfire. It also has the only beachfront RV (recreational vehicle) park. The beach is not surrounded by buildings or houses, despite being near the city.

Hermosa Beach - beautiful, bronzed and buffed beach. A typical day on this path will see hundreds of people on foot, bicycle, skateboard and rollerblades enjoying the sun and surf. The wide and flat sand provides the perfect venue for beach volleyball. Permanent volleyball poles and nets are maintained by the city.

Malibu Surf-rider Beach - Malibu's Surf-rider Beach is a premier surfing beach. It is located on the East coast of Malibu Creek Bridge and is a legendary cultural landmark with some of the best waves in Southern California. Malibu is a way of life for some and an interesting place to visit for others. Since the famous Malibu Country Market is close by, you might catch a glimpse of a celebrity or two here as well.

Santa Monica Beach - a busy, bright pier with food stalls, games arcades, and a shopping mall. The Santa Monica Pier was opened in 1909 and has been used in many films and photographs since. It is a must-see on anyone's agenda.

Muscle Beach - situated on Venice Beach, this is a true gem of an experience for all visitors to LA. It's famous for 'The Pit', an outdoor collection of weights for body builders. The Pit is a favourite for locals and celebrities, such as Kirk Douglas, Clark Gable, Tyrone Power, Jayne Mansfield and Jane Russell, while bodybuilders like Joe Gold (founder of Gold's Gym and World Gym) have used the Pit's resources to sculpt their body and stay fit. The gym features chin bars at various heights, parallel bars, rings, small jungle gyms for children and a padded safe gymnastics area for tumbling.

Zuma Beach, Malibu - one of the most famous and popular beaches in Southern California. The drive down the Pacific Coast Highway is a gorgeous way to take in the views of the scenery.

If you get a bit tired of the sand, head to one of LA's many theme parks. Universal Studios is a movie-based theme park offering thrilling rides, action shows and a backstage tour. It is still a working studio, although visitors won't see much real-life filming. It was founded in 1909 when Carl Laemmle invited the public to observe filmmaking first-hand. A VIP tour is also available for those wanting a more personal tour of the sets and includes all you can eat, private tram rides and a backstage pass.

Adventure: Beach Bum
Destination: Los Angeles

Beverly Hills is known for its lavish estates and beautiful architecture. One famous house in Beverly Hills is Greystone Mansion, the largest mansion that has ever been built in the city. It has the traditional feel of an historic castle with limestone walls and stone courtyards. The house has been used as a set in many popular films, including Indecent Proposal and The Bodyguard.

Visitors are welcome to drive through the wrought iron gates and walk the grounds. You might be able to catch one of the some classical (chamber music) concerts which are sometimes held in the drawing room.

There is a guided tour of a selection of celebrities' homes and it is very popular among tourists. If you don't want to go with a tour group, grab a free map from the tourist office and drive around yourself.

No trip to Hollywood would be complete without seeing the iconic sign - all 50 feet of it - on Mount Lee. It was constructed in 1923 by Harry Chandler. The sign originally read 'Hollywoodland' and was an invitation to all up-and-coming stars to search for their big break in the entertainment industry. During the Great Depression, the sign was left derelict. Eventually, the Hollywood Chamber of Commerce stepped in to repair the sign, but they dropped the last four letters. The sign is best viewed from the corner of Sunset Boulevard and Bronson Avenue, or from Paramount Studios at Melrose Avenue and Gower Street. It is also possible to drive close to the sign and hike even close to it, but remember that most trails get very hot in the summer - so it's best to set off early in the morning or late afternoon.

On Hollywood Boulevard is Grauman's Chinese Theatre, the place where movie greats have made imprints of their hands and feet in the pavement (or 'sidewalk'). Grauman's Theatre has been a landmark of Hollywood for over 75 years. The grand opening of the theatre was in 1927 and, at that time, it was the most impressive theatre opening in motion picture history. The Chinese Theatre is visited by more than four million visitors from all over the world every year and is the most sought-after studio in Hollywood for premieres. Every time there is a premiere, the streets are overrun by fans trying to get autographs and pictures of their favourite celebrities as they arrive for the red carpet walk-ins. The Hollywood Walk of Fame runs right in front of the theatre. To date the imprints of more than 200 of Hollywood's finest hands and feet, such as Marilyn Monroe and Humphrey Bogart, are permanently cast right in the front entrance of the theatre.

Rodeo Drive is worth a visit for shopping. The street set the scene for the famous Pretty Woman movie where Julia Roberts was turned away by snarling sales assistants. Situated between Santa Monica Boulevard and Wilshire Boulevard, Rodeo Drive is a world famous three-block stretch of LA's best shops and boutiques. It is one of the most expensive shopping districts in the world and its shop owners have paid a hefty price tag for real estate there. Bijan, at 420 Rodeo Drive, is the single most expensive shop in the world. Appointments have to be made to shop there and items range from a $50 for a pair of socks to a $50,000 for a suit.

Top. Beverly Wilshire Hotel.
Bottom. Fins Creekside Calabasas.

⇆ Stylish Places to Stay

Pretty Charming: Beverley Wiltshire Hotel.
Setting for the Hollywood blockbuster film Pretty
Woman, where Julia Roberts swims in the 'tub' with
Richard Gere, this hotel is located near to Rodeo
Drive - a shopper's paradise. The Wiltshire is
charming. It has a lovely cocktail bar and rooftop
pool, and decadent rooms. ☆

Fun & Funky: The Standard. Located in downtown
LA, the Standard is a mecca for the young and cool
LA crowd. It really pushes design to its limits. To get
to the toilets you have to walk through a woman's
legs and the reception area has a lady asleep in
a clear tank. Its heated rooftop pool has scarlet
perspex seating pods and matching astroturf. ☆

Seaside Chic: Shutters on the Beach. Located
in Santa Monica, this is LA's only hotel which is
situated directly on the beach. Most rooms are fully
equipped with the latest technology, including
bathroom plasma TVs. It also has a wonderful Ole
Henrikson spa, famed for its lush treatments.

▮ Delicious Places to Eat

Garden Chic: The Ivy. Paparazzi line the pavement
outside The Ivy. On the patio, white tables topped
with potted plants and candles sit near pillow-lined
benches, bordered by a peeling white picket fence.
Food portions are huge. ☆

Grill Chic: Jazz Hal's Bar & Grill. Hal's opened
in 1987 in the heart of Venice, and is an airy and
spacious neighborhood restaurant, serving new
American cuisine in an unpretentious atmosphere.
Cool loft-style and revolving artwork. Live jazz on
Sundays and Mondays.

Fine Cuisine: Fins Creekside Calabasas. Great
for an intimate evening and for those who love varied
seafood. The deserts are particularly excellent, but
the huge portions are not good for your waistline. It
also features live piano on weekdays and R&B and
Jazz trios every weekend. Ask when you reserve
about their special wine evenings.

Adventure: Action Hero
Destination: Las Vegas & Grand Canyon

✈ **Regional Information**

Las Vegas is the most populous city in the state of Nevada and is renowned for shopping, shows, 24 hour drinking, gambling and other forms of adult entertainment. It was established in 1905 and officially became a city in 1911. Today, it is known as 'The Entertainment Capital of the World'. Las Vegas has recently become a glamourous and popular setting for films and TV programmes. However, Las Vegas isn't just about gambling and over-the-top glamour. The surrounding area has some of the South West's most beautiful and stunning scenery. These areas offer some great action adventures, including golf, skiing, cycling across Death Valley, rock climbing, walking and hiking, among others. But what makes this area stand out so much is the availability of everything; you can do anything, whenever you want, 24 hours a day, 7 days a week. There is nowhere quite like it in the world.

If you intend to visit Las Vegas for a few days, you can stroll through mega-shopping complexes and opulent resorts. If you intend to stay a week, you will probably catch most of the city's sights and shows as well as get the chance to explore further afield to Lake Mead, the Hoover Dam or an overnight excursion to the Grand Canyon.

Getting to Las Vegas is easy. McCarren Airport is only 30 minutes drive from The Strip and is serviced by many domestic routes from other US cities as well as by direct routes from the UK.

Las Vegas itself is really divided up into two cities, The Strip, and the older downtown area. Although most of the sights and glam hotels are focused around The Strip, downtown is famed for its 'serious' casinos and original buildings.

Walking The Strip and visiting each opulent hotel casino is enough to keep you entertained for a full day or more. The Strip itself is 4.5 miles long and stretches the length of Las Vegas Boulevard. At the north end is the magnificent Wynn mega-resort (with over 2,700 rooms) and at the south end is Planet Hollywood's Aladdin. One of The Strip's most appealing experiences is a trip on a gondola at the Venetian hotel. This is a romantic replica of a Venetian canal with hand-painted frescoes, bridges and piazzas (squares), and is well worth a visit. For an action thrill, the Venetian also has an impressive indoor climbing wall, where you can book a lesson with a professional instructor.

The Luxor hotel is named after Egypt's ancient city. You can't fail to miss its huge pyramid, a shrine to Egyptian art and architecture. It is 30 storeys high and its apex beacon, the world's most powerful, sends a shaft of blue light 10 miles into space. Across the front of the hotel lie sphinx and a sandstone obelisk - stunning replicas of the real thing.

The Mandalay Bay hotel is as grand as they come. Its stage has been graced by some of the world's best-known celebrities and Red Square, with its solid icebar (with a huge selection of frozen cocktails) is pretty special. The outstanding feature here is the Shark Reef, which acts as an educational conservation facility and is home to a huge aquarium of marine life. There is even a shallow petting pool for those wanting a more personal experience.

The lion habitat at the MGM Grand is quite an unusual experience. Its habitat is right in the middle of the casino, with visitors peering through the reinforced glass to see the lions sleeping, eating and playing.

You cannot fail to see the Stratosphere Tower. It's the tallest building in the USA west of the Mississippi River. At 350 metres tall, it offers thrill-seekers a real rush: riders are strapped into completely exposed seats that zip up to the pinnacle, while Insanity spins riders out over the Tower's edge. There is also a revolving restaurant and lounge at the top, just in case you fancy an extra spin.

The Las Vegas Cyber Speedway and Speed is a must for adrenaline junkies. It's housed just inside the NASCAR café. The Indy car simulators, with 7 metre wraparound screens, are mounted on hydraulics and sound very authentic. The 15 speaker sound system would even excite real Formula One drivers. Speed is an electromagnetic roller coaster that slingshots riders through the casino's hotel sign at speeds of up to 70 mph.

Other activities to keep you entertained in Las Vegas include golf, skiing, water sports and hiking.

Golf - there are dozens of golf courses in Las Vegas Valley, most within 16 km of the Strip. Unless you can hustle together $30,000.00 up front plus $500.00 a month for membership of a private club, you'll be playing on a public course. Reserve your tee-off time a week in advance.

Skiing - novice skiers will be thrilled by the downhill at the Lee Canyon ski and snowboarding area on Charleston Peak, in the Humboldt-Toiyabe National Forest, about 80 km Northwest of Las Vegas.

Water sports - for boating and water-skiing, slither into your wetsuit and head over to Lake Mead, about 50 km east of Las Vegas. You can even scuba dive here. The lake's 880 km of shoreline also offers plenty of sunbathing spots.

Adventure: Action Hero
Destination: Las Vegas &
Grand Canyon

Hiking - Red Rock Canyon National Conservation Area is great for hiking. The area is about 30 km west of Las Vegas and has multi-coloured sandstone scenery which climbers and hikers find it difficult to resist. The Humboldt-Toiyabe National Forest, north west of the city, features Charleston Peak and trails that wind through pine forests and desert scrub. Camping is allowed at both parks.

The famous Grand Canyon is one of the best trips for an adrenaline thrills. You can see the canyon in a day, or if you would prefer not to rush, you can stay there overnight. The canyon is one of the USA's most famous sights and is one of the world's top attractions. It is 277 miles long and 10 miles wide. It features many peaks and rims and has the Colorado River through it. The Grand Canyon is split up into the North and South Rim. About 90% of visitors go into the South Rim, and stay at camping grounds or at one of the ranches. The rim is a very scenic 33 mile road which is rich in wilderness and beauty. If you are really into adventure then spend a few days here exploring the inner gorges and walking the banks of the Colorado River (head to Grand Canyon Village for information and amenities). The North Rim of the canyon is much more remote. If you are looking to escape the crowds then this is where you should head. Most visitor facilities are around the North Rim Visitors centre. For excellent canyon views and walking paths head to Bright Angel point, which will take your breath away. The Roaring Springs are a popular day's hike or a mule ride destination - perfect for adventure travellers!

The Hoover Dam, 30 miles Southeast of Vegas is another sight worth visiting. It is a concrete gravity-arch dam in the Black Canyon of the Colorado River, on the border between Arizona and Nevada. You can take a helicopter tour over the Hoover Dam followed by a day or an overnight stay with in a tent at a ranch. The flight over the dam offers stunning views of the dam and of Lake Mead (the resevoir behind it). Once landed on the ranch (if you are on an organised tour) you will be escorted into your wigwam and offered food 'à la Cowboy'. The day usually completes with learning how to lasso a horse and ride on horseback.

Finally, Death Valley (not as scary as it sounds) covers a huge area of national park (50,00 square miles) and is the lowest elevation in the USA. During the summer, temperatures soar above 120°F (49°C) and is almost a near death experience in itself. Many travellers choose to cross Death Valley due to the wonderful rock formations, rich colour and fabulous sunsets and sunrises. Try it if you dare!

Top. Bellagio, Las Vegas. **Bottom.** Voodoo Lounge Terrace.

⤴ Stylish Places to Stay

Italian Elegance: The Bellagio. Inspired by the beauty of the Italian lakes, this $1.6 billion Vegas hotel is opulent and legendary. From the 18 ft ceiling lobby, to the travelling gallery of fine art, not to mention the private poolside cabanas, this place oozes charm and decadence. The dancing fountains draw crowds daily, outside the front, so if you are not staying at the hotel, you can still enjoy its entertainment. ⭐

Boutique Chic: Skylofts @ MGM Grand. Located on top of the MGM Grand, each of the 51 lofts features 24 ft floor-to-ceiling windows which providing dramatic views of The Strip.

Ranch Charm: Red Rock Ranch. This hotel is only minutes from The Strip, but it feels like a million miles away! This working cattle ranch makes room for families who want a fun experience amid the peaceful wilderness of the Gros Ventre Mountains, east of Grand Teton National Park. They have nine comfortable log cabins, live music and horseback riding to keep you entertained.

🍽 Delicious Places to Eat

Magical Charm: Voodoo Lounge. This lounge is a great rooftop venue with an excellent menu serving innovative cocktails and modern American cuisine. Try one of the unusual 'Witch Doctor' cocktails. ⭐

French Fancies: Joël Robuchon. Legendary French Chef Joël Robuchon has come out of retirement to open his very first and only fine dining French restaurant in the USA. You can choose to sit at a table, but the real action takes place at the granite topped U-shaped bar that offers great views of the chefs at work in the kitchen.

Nouvelle American: Aureole. Chef Charlie Palmer is making quite an impact with inspired American dishes and extensive wine list. Reservations are essential here.

Focus On...
Living it up in Miami

Miami is an eclectic urban mix of beach socialites, Latin Americans and holidaymakers. It's known as the 'Gateway of the Americas' because of its strong economic ties to Latin America. As much as 60% of its residents speak Spanish. With its wild nightclubs, sandy beaches and exquisite shopping - Miami has much to offer. South Beach is where it all happens.

Visiting on or around July 4th (American Independence day) is a real treat. The city comes alive with holidaymakers from all over the USA, and in downtown Miami they host an incredible fireworks display and party-on until dawn. Not that Miamians need an excuse to party, as every night there seems to be a party in town. You can relax in the tropical gardens at the Sky Bar (The Shore Club Hotel) or hire a private table at Privé - an exclusive nightclub and lounge which is famous for entertaining celebrities.

Dining out in style is also a typical Miamian past time. Have a lazy lunch at one of the beach hotels (such as The Delano), or dress up for an evening meal at one of the themed restaurants like Tantra (which has exotic Middle Eastern decor, a live grass floor and a waterwall).

South Beach is legendary for its shopping. Go and shop in the huge malls (like Bal Harbour) where you can buy every designer brand from Versace to Cavalli. The Miami climate is hot for most of the year, so the air-conditioning in the shopping malls are a welcome comfort.

Wherever you go make sure you dress well. The Miamians have a penchant for dressing up, and looking good is endemic, so don't be surprised if you see people twice your age looking half your age!

Opposite page. South Beach, Miami.

ⓘ Stylish Essentials

General Tourist Information
www.usa.worldweb.com

TSA Website
www.tsa.gov

Visa Information
www.travel.state.gov/visa

UK Embassy in the USA
www.britainusa.com

Airlines

Silverjet
www.flysilverjet.com
T. 0844 855 0111 (UK Reservations)

Virgin Atlantic
www.virgin-atlantic.com
T. 0870 380 2007 (UK Reservations)

British Airways
www.britishairways.com
T. 0870 850 9850 (UK Reservations)

BMI
www.flybmi.com
T. 0870 6070 222 (Long-haul reservations)

New York

JFK Airport John F. Kennedy International Airport (JFK)
JFK, in Queens (at the South end of the Van Wyck Expressway), primarily handles international flights.
www.kennedyairport.com

LaGuardia Airport (LGA)
LaGuardia, also in Queens (on the Grand Central Parkway), mainly handles domestic flights. If you're flying in from anywhere in the U.S, chances are you'll come through here.

Newark International Airport (EWR)
Newark, in Newark, New Jersey, handles both domestic and international flights.

Empire State Building
T. +1 212 736 3100
Open: Daily 09.30 am - midnight

Statue Of Liberty
T. +1 212 269 5755 Liberty Island
T. +1 212 363 3200 Recorded Info
The Circle-Line-Statue of Liberty ferry from Battery Park runs every 30mins.
Open: 9.30 am – 3.30 pm during summer.

Central Park
www.centralparknyc.org
T. +1 212 360 3444 (info)
Open: 6.00 am – 1.00 am

Shops

Vintage New York
482 Broome St at Wooster St 10013
www.vintagenewyork.com
T. +1 212 226 9463 (info)
Open: Mon-Sat 11.00 am – 9.00 pm,
Sun Noon - 9.00 pm

Saks Fifth Avenue
www.saksfifthavenue.com

American Apparel
121 Spring St 10012
www.americanapparel.net
Open: Mon-Thu 10.00 am – 8.00 pm,
Fri-Sat 10.00 am – 9.00 pm,
Sun 11.00 am – 8.00 pm

Apple Store
103 Prince St
T. +1 212 226 3126 (info)
Open: Mon-Sat 10.00 am – 8.00pm,
Sun 11.00 am – 7.00 pm

Broadway Tourist Information
www.broadway.com

Hotel Gansevoort
www.hotelgansevoort.com
T. +1 212 206 6700 (info)

SoHo House
www.sohohouseny.com
T. +1 212 627 9800 (info)

The Library
www.libraryhotel.com
T. +1 212-983 4500

Spice Market
403 W. 13th St., New York, NY
10014 at Ninth Ave.
T. +1 212 675 2322

Pastis
9 9th Ave, New York, NY
10014+1203
T. +1 212 929 4844

Strip House
13 E 12th St, New York, NY
T. +1 212 328-0000

Los Angeles

Airports

Los Angeles International Airport (LAX)
www.lawa.org/lax/

Tourist Information Office
LA visitors centre, 685 figueroa st
T. +1213 689 8822
Open: Mon-Fri, 9.00 am – 5.00 pm

Hollywood City Pass for TV shows and celebrity Sighting
www.citypass.com

Venice Beach
Venice Beach centered around the Venice Pier at Washington Street.
Exit I-405 at Washington and go West

Dockweiler Beach
Located at 12000 Vista del Mar in Playa del Rey.
To get there, take I-105 West to its end at Imperial Highway and turn right.

Manhattan Beach
The Manhattan Beach pier is at the end of Manhattan Beach Boulevard.

Santa Monica Beach
To reach Santa Monica State Beach, take I-10 West to where it ends at Pacific Coast Highway (CA 1).

Zuma Beach
30000 Pacific Coast Highway,
Malibu CA 90265

Fins Creekside Calabasas
23504 Calabasas Rd
Calabasas, CA 91302
T. +1 818 223 3467
Opens: Mon-Thu 11.00 am – 10.00 pm, Fri 11.00 am – 11.00 pm,
Sat 5.00 pm – 11.00 pm,
Sun 10.30 pm – 9.00 pm

Griffith Park Observatory
4800 Western Heritage Way, CA
90027,
www.griffithobs.org
T. +1 1323 6641181

Graumanns Chinese Theatre
6925 Hollywood Boulevard, between
Highland and La Brea Avenues, CA
90028,
www.manntheatres.com
T. +1 323 4613331

The Walk of Fame
6801 Hollywood Blvd, Los Angeles,
CA 90028

Tour of the Stars Home
www.starlinetours.com

Beverly Wilshire Hotel
Wilshire Boulevard at Rodeo Drive,
Beverly Hills CA 90212 USA
www.fourseasons.com/beverlywilshire
T. +1 310 858 2399

The Standard
550 South Flower 6th Street
Los Angeles CA 90071
www.standardhotel.com
T. +1 213 892 8080

Shutters on the Beach
1 Pico Blvd, Santa Monica CA 90405
www.shuttersonthebeach.com
T. +1 310 458 0030

The Ivy
113.N Robertson Blvd.
Los Angeles, CA 90048
T. +1 310 274 8303
Opens: Mon-Sat 11.30 am – 11.00 pm
Sun. 10.30 am – 10.30 pm

Hal's Bar & Grill
1349 Abbot Kinney Blvd
www.halsbarandgrill.com
T. +1 310 396 3105
Opens: 11.30 am – 2.00 am daily

Universal Studios
100 Universal City Plaza, Universal
City, CA 91608,
www.universalstudioshollywood.com
T. +1 3109 790114
T. (VIP experience) 800 864 8377

Las Vegas & Grand Canyon

Las Vegas MCcarren Airport
www.mccarran.com
T. +1 702 261-5211

Tourist Information Website
www.visitlasvegas.com

Grand Canyon Express
www.airvegas.com

Pappillon Helicopter flights
www.scenic.com

Heli USA Grand Canyon tours
www.heliusa.com
T. +1 702.736.8787

**Grand Canyon Village
Tourist Information Centre**
T. +1 928 638 7875

North Rim Visitors Centre
T. +1 928 638 7864
Open: 8.00 – 6.00 pm daily

Stratosphere Tower
2000 Las Vegas Blvd S
www.stratospherehotel.com
T. +1 702 380 7777 (info)
Open: Sun-Thu 10.00 am – 1.00 am,
Fri-Sat 10.00 am – 2.00 am

**Las Vegas Cyber Speedway
& Speed**
2535 Las Vegas Blvd S
www.nascarcafelasvegas.com
T. +1 702 734 7223 (info)
Open: Speedway:
Sun-Thu 10.00 am – 12.00 am,
Fri-Sat 10.00 am – 1:00 am

The Bellagio
3600 S. Las Vegas Blvd. Las Vegas,
NV 89109
www.bellagio.com
T. +1 888-987-6667 (Room
Reservations)
T. +1 702-693-7111 (General
Information)

Sky Lofts @ MGM Grand
3799 Las Vegas Boulevard South,
Las Vegas NV 89109
www.skyloftsmgmgrand.com
T. +1-702 891 3832

Red Rock Ranch
11011 W. Charleston
Las Vegas, NV 89135
www.redrocklasvegas.com
T. +1 702 797 7777

Voodoo Lounge
3700 W Flamingo Road
Las Vegas, 89109
T. +1 702 252 7777

Joel Robuchon
MGM Grand Hotel, 3799 Las Vegas
Blvd S, Las Vegas, NV 89109
T. +1 702 891-7777

Aureole restaurant
Mandalay Bay Hotel, 3950 Las Vegas
Blvd S, Las Vegas, NV 89119
www.aureolelv.com
T. +1 702 632 7777
Opens: Mon - Sun 6.00 am – 10.30 pm

Miami

General Information
www.visitflorida.com

The Delano Hotel
1685 Collins Ave.
Miami Beach, FL 33139
www.delano-hotel.com
T. +1 305 672 2000

Prive
136 Collins Avenue, Miami Beach
www.theopiumgroup.com
T. +1 305 531 5535

Sanctuary Hotel
www.sanctuarysobe.com
T. +1 305 673 5455

Tantra Restaurant & Lounge
1445 Pennsylvania Avenue
Miami Beach, Florida FL 33139
www.tantrarestaurant.com
T. +1 305 672 4765

Bal Harbour Shops
9700 Collins Ave, Bal Harbour
www.balharbourshops.com
T. +1 305 866 0311

Tips and advice

Visas

Once you have researched and planned your trip, you need to make sure you have the right Visa for that country. Some countries (especially those in the EU for the UK travellers) don't require them, some are issued on landing and others need to be planned way in advance. Make sure you don't get stuck and check with the consulate or embassy of the country in question. Also check out www.fco.gov.uk for travel notes and advice before you fly.

Vaccinations

Everyone hates them, but they are a necessity for most travellers. Some countries even require proof of vaccines before entry is permitted, and you will need to carry a medical card with you. It is your responsibility to make sure you receive detailed medical advice in time before your departure. Your local GP should be able to advise you on which vaccines you need for any particular country. You can always check out www.dh.gov.uk to find out yourself, and if you can't stand needles, you may want to re-route your trip to a destination that doesn't have any vaccine requirements.

Insurance

We hope you will never need it. But it's the first thing you will need if things go wrong. There are so many companies on the market that offer different levels of insurance; it's a minefield selecting the right one for your trip. Our advice is, make sure you have adequate cover for the full cost of cancellation/curtailment of your trip, all your bags, belongings, cash and medical bills. Don't be underinsured, be realistic. It's also a good idea to select an insurance policy that will cover you for any specialist activities, such as scuba diving. Read the small print and make sure you are covered for everything.

Staying Healthy

Nobody wants to be running to the toilet every five minutes or be hauled up in bed with a flu bug for a week when they are travelling. Being sick can be disastrous for any adventure, it can ruin your plans and can cost you a small fortune if you have to cancel trips, hotels or change flights. Tips to staying healthy are very simple. Make sure you are well hydrated and drink plenty of bottled or filtered water every day, and wash or sanitize your hands before eating. If you are uncertain about what you are eating, or if the food reaches the table before you have finished ordering, then don't eat it. Don't risk your health, or the trip of your lifetime, by being polite. For further information about healthy travel, ask your GP.

Get signed up
Frequent flyer programmes for hotels and airlines are usually free to join and mean that you can earn valuable points while you travel. Once you have earned sufficient miles you can use them for upgrades, hotel rooms and flights. The best frequent flyer programme we have found is Star Alliance which includes a good variety of airlines and hotels, (www.staralliance.com).

Flexible planning
You will have greater flexibility and control over your choice of places to stay if you don't pre-book your accommodation. On arrival, we have previously reviewed local hotels by taking a taxi around different ones and asking to see the rooms and facilities before we stay. We have often managed to get a substantial room discount off the published rate by speaking to the reservation manager in person. This works especially well if you arrive late at night, as the hotel would rather fill the room than leave it empty.

Transfers
If you have booked a business class or first class ticket, some airlines offer free transfers both from home and on arrival. This can save you money and time in finding your way to your hotel. The best airline for this service we have experienced is Emirates, (www.emirates.com).

Meeting other travellers
Whether you are taking an extended trip or a short break, the best way to meet other like-minded travellers is to join in a course or special interest activity, such as wine tasting or scuba diving. You will get to know other travellers with similar interests and opinions. It's also a good way of sharing travelling tips while you are travelling.

Meeting the Locals
If you want more than just the tourist blurb you get from some organised excursions, opting for a locally run guided tour may suit you better. Always ask your concierge or local tourist information centre if they recommend any local guides, as often they are not employed by an agency but work independently. They normally have extensive knowledge of the local area and the tour will probably be more personal. You will also do your bit in helping local people staying financially independent.

For more information and travel advice visit
www.luxurybackpackers.com

Competition

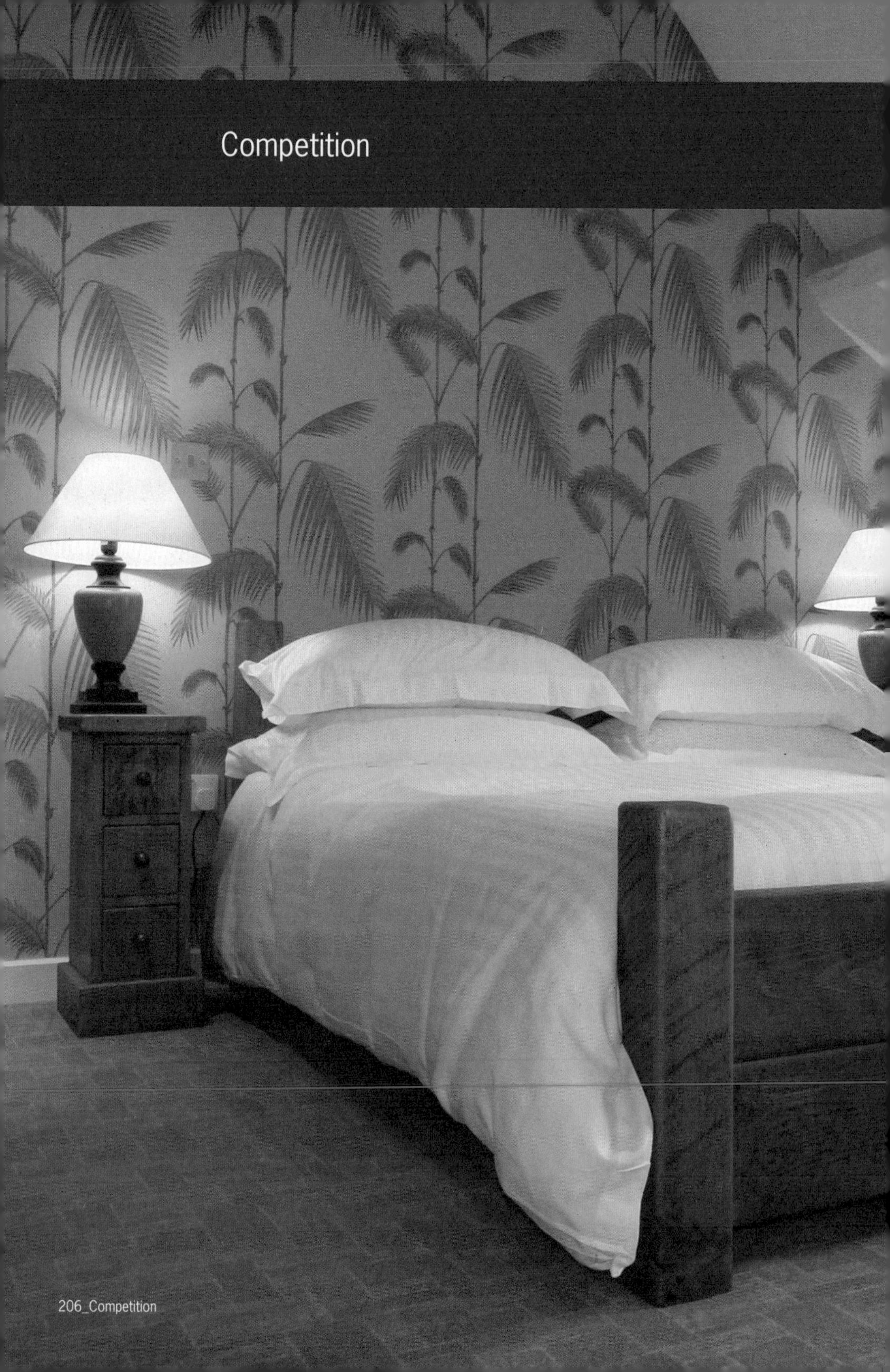

It's time to escape the city, pack your backpacks and head to the wonderful Lake District. There are plenty of outdoor adventures on your doorstep here, such as hiking, climbing, or soaking up the traditional English hospitality with some tea and scones. Luxury Backpackers have teamed up with 'Moss Grove Organic Hotel' in Grasmere to offer an exclusive 2-night stay in an executive room. All rooms have hand made beds and furnishings, spa baths, flat screen television, free high speed internet access, Bose home entertainment systems, complimentary free-trade tea and coffee facilities, and organic biscuits. A wonderful farmhouse style breakfast is also included.*

*Terms and Conditions apply

For your chance to win, answer this question...

Which famous English romantic poet was inspired by Lake Grasmere?

Send your answers to...

info@luxurybackpackers.com

Money travelling further in fighting climate change

As responsible travellers, most of us wouldn't dream of dumping our litter on pristine beaches, or staying in a hotel that poured waste chemicals straight into the sea. Yet there is one type of pollution that we all contribute to – the pollution that is causing climate change. The atmosphere that surrounds our beautiful planet is very thin, like a layer of tissue around a beach ball. One vital function is to keep 'space-ship earth' a pleasant temperature to live on. Sunlight passes through the atmosphere and heats the ground, and some of this heat radiating back out to space is trapped by 'greenhouse gases', keeping the global average temperature at a pleasant 14.4°C. The problem is that humans have become very effective at adding more and more greenhouse gas to the atmosphere. Because this is invisible, and its impact difficult to spot at first, it has been all too easy to ignore. Our global economy has grown up turning a blind eye to its carbon pollution.

Climate Care was set up a decade ago to do something about this. Our founder, Mike Mason, saw that the key to greening the global economy was to give carbon emissions a price – polluters have to pay, and reducers get rewarded. This is the principle behind 'carbon offsetting' – buying carbon reductions to compensate for your own unavoidable emissions. You measure your impact on the climate and pay Climate Care to reduce the same amount, through funding green energy projects around the world. Carbon offsetting is not an excuse to keep on polluting, but an essential tool to deal with the carbon you can't avoid, just as recycling deals with unavoidable waste.

For example one person's return flight from London to New York will produce an estimated 1.5 tonnes of CO2, which will cost around £12 to offset. This may seem very cheap, but there are so many opportunities where small amounts of money can fund large reductions. Put simply, credible carbon offsets direct your money wherever in the world it can make the biggest impact. For example in India a simple water pump, being promoted by a local organisation with funding from Climate Care,

is transforming the lives of rural farmers such as Mr Pyari. Powered by foot, it replaces diesel pumps that are costly to hire, and not reliably available to the most poor. The result?: Mr Pyari has healthier crops, twice the annual income and he is no longer forced to leave his family for 6 months a year to find work in the city. The switch saves the climate around half a tonne of CO_2 per year – for a cost of only 1,260 rupees per pump (£15). It will take a solar panel on a UK home 2,000 years to make the same carbon savings that the treadle pump project will make in a single year with the same investment (around £12,000 per 2kWh panel). If we are serious about tackling climate change we have to help fund reductions abroad as well as working hard to reducing our carbon footprints at home.

When you buy your offset you want to know that a real reduction in pollution has been made which wouldn't have happened otherwise. All Climate Care's projects are accredited to an internationally recognised standard - an independent body approves each project and checks that the carbon savings are made. By using a basket of different projects – wind energy, water pumps, efficient cookstoves – we make sure that the success of your offset doesn't depend on any one in particular.

Thanks to our customers we're starting to make a significant impact – we have delivered over 1 million tonnes of carbon savings, and in 2008 expect to fund savings equivalent to 1% of the UK's total annual carbon emissions.

Want to take responsibility for your unavoidable carbon impact? And support the global 'green energy' revolution?

www.climatecare.org

Sponsored by...

Acknowledgments

Adventure Index

A project such as this is a major team effort and relies on the help and generosity of many fantastic people all over the world. Jill & Carlo would like to personally thank...

Kerry Dennison, Jonathan Lorie, Sam Haslam, Shuey Chowdhury, Steph Tomkinson, Sam Anson, Abigail Gallagher, Nicola Osmond-Evans, ClimateCare, Nicky Black, Steve Ricketts, Andrew Goodwin, Tarquin Cooper, all the staff at Komodomedia and all of our friends and family who have supported and believed in us throughout the production of this book.

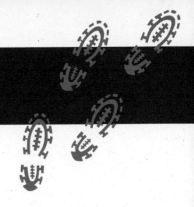

ISBN 978-0-9557397-0-5
Published by Luxury Backpackers Ltd 2007 in the UK

Luxury Backpackers Ltd Reg. No. 5661479
Address for Luxury Backpackers can be found on
www.luxurybackpackers.com

Printed by MRT Response in the UK

Copy-editor: Jonathan Lorie
Designer: Steph Tomkinson